JOHN WARNER BARBER'S
VIEWS OF CONNECTICUT TOWNS
1834–36

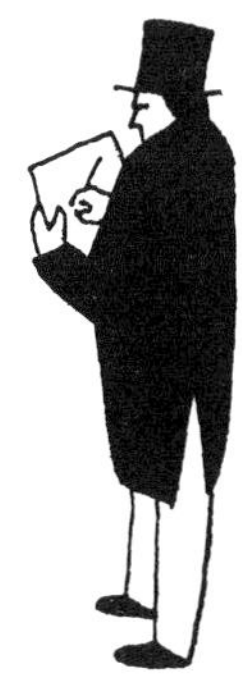

JOHN WARNER BARBER'S VIEWS OF CONNECTICUT TOWNS 1834–36

Edited by

CHRISTOPHER P. BICKFORD
J. BARD MCNULTY

THE ACORN CLUB
The Connecticut Historical Society

Thirty-third Publication of the Acorn Club

ISBN 0–94078–98–3

CONTENTS

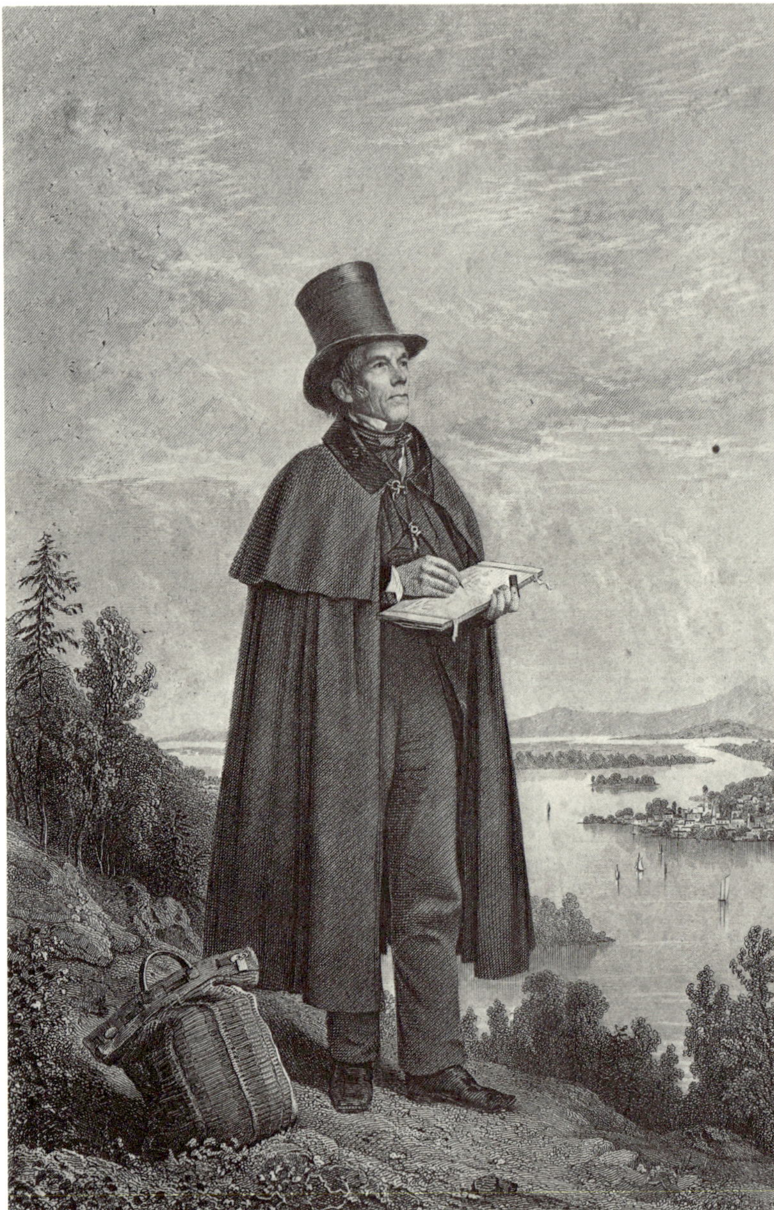

John W. Barber.

FOREWORD

The Acorn Club and The Connecticut Historical Society are pleased to present these views of early nineteenth century Connecticut by John Warner Barber (1798–1885). Barber loved history and his native state. Over a three-year period from 1834 to 1836, he traveled to nearly every Connecticut town taking pencil sketches which he later turned into ink washes and then into wood engravings for inclusion in his *Connecticut Historical Collections* published in 1836. These represent our earliest known images of many towns; they document the changing face of our state at the early stages of rapid industrialization. Although a few of Barber's ink washes have been reproduced before, most of those appearing in this volume have never been published before.

The John Warner Barber collection of pencil sketches and ink washes came to the Society in 1953 as a gift of Houghton Bulkeley who probably acquired them from his father, Governor Morgan G. Bulkeley. An appendix to this volume provides a checklist of the surviving pencil sketches, ink washes, and wood blocks. Not all towns are represented in this volume because not all of Barber's ink washes have survived.

This project was initiated and carried out by the Acorn Club, an organization founded in 1899 to publish books of enduring value about Connecticut history. The brief town entries, prepared and initialed by club members whose full names can be found in the back of the book, describe the location and angle of the view and the changes that have occurred to each scene since Barber's visit more than 150 years ago. The club members wish to thank the many local residents who have assisted them in preparing their brief essays.

July 1990

Robert Ewing, President, The Connecticut Historical Society
Floyd M. Shumway, President, The Acorn Club

JOHN WARNER BARBER: HISTORIAN FOR THE PLAIN PEOPLE

IN 1837, SOON AFTER John Warner Barber published the second edition of *The Connecticut Historical Collections*, he wrote to a Worcester, Massachusetts publisher to discuss a similar volume on Massachusetts. Working with Edward R. Lambert of New Haven, Barber proposed to retain control over the entire text as well as the illustrations. Despite the fact that these two men lacked any formal historical training and were not natives of the Commonwealth, Barber was still insistent on serving as author as well as illustrator; he explained:

> In our apprehension, most of our distinguished literary men are improper persons to write a work of the kind we propose, they move and act in a higher sphere than the great mass of the common people. They would probably reject many things which we should wish inserted and instead thereof insert facts which might be valuable and proper in a formal history, but to the great body of readers would be dry and uninteresting and fatal to its popularity among the common people.

Barber maintained in the letter that because of the great success of the Connecticut book, "we know from demonstration what is popular among Connecticut people, and from this we judge what would be popular in Massachusetts."[1]

Barber proved correct and *The Massachusetts Historical Collections* did become a bestseller. The critical reception to the book in Boston was another matter, however. The Boston *Courier* issued a scathing review which dismissed the book and urged the author to return to the farm. "The book is amusing enough to a certain class of readers, but we can hardly pronounce it a valuable work." The information may be accurate, admitted the reviewer, but the obscure facts which Barber chose to include would have been better left to lie undisturbed in complete repose. The illustrations were found to be little better. The engravings were described as wood cuts, "badly drawn, and most clumsily engraved; if such botch-work can be called engraving." After thanking Barber for his industry and for making an entertaining book, the disdainful reviewer

1. John Warner Barber, Account Book Number 2, Beinecke Library, Yale University.

suggested that the author would have made a greater contribution to humanity by chopping wood, digging up briers, and mowing down thistles. "Heaven save us from such embellishments," the reviewer concluded.[2]

By the standards of fine wood engraving of the 19th century and compared to the masters of historical writing of the period such as Jared Sparks and George Bancroft, John Warner Barber obviously falls short. But that is to miss the point and to mistake his importance. John Warner Barber deliberately cultivated—indeed may have created—the market for popular history and he may well be the first popular American historian on any large scale. He was one of the first artists to carry out a comprehensive visual survey of an entire state. The better known Benson Lossing who came along a decade and a half later credits Barber with providing him with the inspiration to write illustrated histories and historical guidebooks for a wide audience. Let us then look at John Warner Barber, examine his work, and try to appreciate this engraver-historian within the framework of his own times.

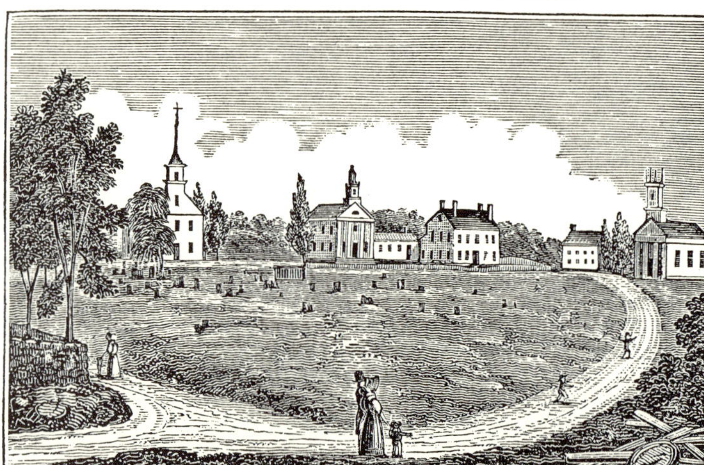

John Warner Barber's Wood Engraving of Church Hill, New Canaan showing, from the right, the Lutheran church built originally as an Episcopal church in 1834, the 1825 Town Hall now the New Canaan Historical Society, the parsonage for the Congregational church, a former academy now a private residence, and, at far left, the Congregational church which was replaced in 1840.

2. A copy of this review dated May ?, 1839 was clipped from the newspaper by Barber and pasted in Account Book Number 3, Fairfield Historical Society.

John Warner Barber was born in Windsor in 1798, the second of six children of Elijah and Mary Warner Barber.[3] Elijah Barber was a farmer of modest circumstances who worked the land, made bricks, and, in the spring, like many residents in the Valley he fished the Connecticut River for shad. When Elijah died in 1812 a major burden fell on John Warner who was obliged—or so he later claimed—to do more farm chores and "to turn up brick in a brick-yard and pound clothes for the women on washing day." Describing his upbringing later in life, John Warner Barber never admitted to any formal schooling as if to emphasize his native talent, but a little bound volume three and one half inches square of crudely drawn pen and ink sketches now in the collections at Beinecke Library were done at an academy at Windsor in 1808 taught by a Dr. James L. Phelps. How long Barber studied at the Windsor Academy is unclear, but it appears that he was far from being completely self-educated. In describing his childhood to his collaborator Henry Howe, Barber acknowledged the influence of the Bible and such illustrated books as Bunyan's *Pilgrims Progress*, the *New England Primer* and Mrs. Barbauld's *Hymns*. One chapbook owned by John Warner Barber was *Lazy Lawrence* which was purchased in Hartford in 1806. A set of pen and ink drawings executed in 1808 and another series done sometime around 1812 both undoubtedly copied from chapbooks demonstrate that Barber's imagination was stirred by the simple woodcut illustrations that appeared in children's books of the time. The little bound sketchbooks were Barber's attempts to create his own children's books on historical subjects.

In Barber's 15th year, he was apprenticed to Abner Reed, a noted engraver of bank notes who had returned to East Windsor in 1811. For a time young John Warner combined farming tasks in the Reed household with the work expected of an engraver's apprentice: binding, pasting and trimming copy, scouring and burnishing plates, coloring plates, filing blocks, and drawing. A diary begun in 1813 demonstrates that by 1814 Barber had ceased to work on ordinary household chores and had become a valuable craftsman in Reed's shop.[4] Barber

3. Henry H. Townshend, "John W. Barber, Illustrator and Historian," *Papers of the New Haven Colony Historical Society*, X, 1951, 313–336.

4. The diary is in the collections of the New Haven Colony Historical Society.

remained with Reed for seven years and on September 1, 1819 received a letter of endorsement.

> This may certify that the bearer, Mr. John Warner Barber, has served a regular and faithful apprenticeship with me at the business of Engraving, and I cheerfully recommend him as a good workman, especially at historical and wood engraving, and as a young man of unblemished moral character; and as meriting encouragement.[5]

John Warner Barber later claimed that he alone among Reed's apprentices chose to learn wood engraving, a technique well suited for book illustration. It is striking in the testimonial that Reed describes Barber not simply as an accomplished wood engraver but as an historical engraver, someone with imagination and interest in the past as well as with technical skills. Clearly, Barber had demonstrated a desire to make a mark as an illustrator of historical books and pamphlets as well as an engraver of bill heads, trade cards and bank notes. Barber left Reed's shop on Dec. 7, 1820 and moved to Hartford in search of work.

It has been said of Barber that over the next 65 years until his death in 1885, he compiled and illustrated no fewer than 34 books and assisted in printing another 84 books. This is probably a conservative estimate. A daily diary which he religiously kept from 1813 until 1885 would undoubtedly reveal, if it were carefully studied, a still greater output. Barber embodied well into his 80s the Protestant work ethic. Clearly he did not waste his time writing extensive diary entries or pursuing leisurely activities.

In his role as author, publisher and original printmaker, Barber's work falls into two broad categories: historical and religious studies, though he was sometimes able to unite these concerns, as with *Historical Religious Events* issued in 1828. Abner Reed, a deacon in the congregational church, obviously took seriously the expectation that an apprentice's master would guide the moral development of his charge. Barber became a member of the same church. In later life, he stated that he "considered it a favorable circumstance that he had been a member of the family of Deacon Reed, where Christian

5. Townshend, 317.
6. Townshend, 324.

rules were adopted and where its heads felt an interest in the religious welfare of those under their charge."[6]

Barber's first religious publication was produced in 1814, a year after he was apprenticed to Reed—a version of Bunyan's *Pilgrim's Progress* issued as a metamorphosis, a single folded sheet in which flaps are lifted to tell the story of moral progress. Barber brought out other editions in 1819, 1822, 1826, 1840 and in three other undated editions. While working in Hartford, Barber published a separate engraving on copper, "A Miniature of the World in the 19th Century," which is said to have been used by American missionaries in converting the Queen of the Sandwich Islands to Christianity.

In his religious views, Barber held to an evangelical view of Christianity, what he called the "apostle's creed." In his diary for each sabbath, Barber would break his habit of writing one line entries and note the church he attended, the officiating minister, and the text of the sermon. He attended services in every denomination: Unitarian, Swedenborgian, Baptist, Wesleyan, Roman Catholic, Free Church, Episcopal, African. In 1844 he joined the "primitive methodists." As one writer has noted, Barber was deeply religious—perhaps even mystical, but he was not orthodox.

Driven by his deep sense of morality, Barber also became involved in various social causes such as the anti-masonic movement, the temperance movement, and abolition. His diary notes when William Lloyd Garrison and other abolitionists appeared in New Haven. In 1831 his diary also records that he was one of only four New Haven citizens who voted in a town meeting in favor of a Black college in the city. His pamphlet on the Amistad case issued in 1840 expressed his strong conviction that the black captives on board the Amistad who rose up and took over the ship should be given their freedom. Concern about racial prejudice led Barber to include an illustration describing an effort to drive a Black tailor out of Hartford around 1814 in his *Picture Preacher* published in 1880.

Beginning in the early 1820s John Warner Barber began to provide illustrations to various historical books and pamphlets such as *The Code of 1650* published by Silas Andrus in 1822.

7. Donald C. O'Brien, "John Warner Barber: A Connecticut Engraver," *Imprint*, vol. 4, no. 1, 21.

After providing engravings for *A History of the American Revolution* in 1824, Barber became an author in his own right with *Historical Scenes in the United States* published in 1827 and *Interesting Events in the History of the United States* in 1828. Just as the illustrations to these publications were simple, uncomplicated compositions without subtlety, the text of Barber's historical publications was straightforward and direct. His literary style was, according to Henry Townshend, "forcible from its simplicity and directness. Facts are facts and so stated."[7] If Barber was no great literary stylist, he was also no historical researcher. He called himself a compiler and as we shall see he found and took his material from any available source. In a preface to an account of religious events he wrote in 1833, Barber noted that in his role as compiler "he has generally confined himself to the bare relation of facts as he found them, leaving his readers to draw their own inferences and conclusions." Quoting from another source, Barber said that no apology was needed for the "free use which has been made of the labors of others." Compilers are "licensed pillagers" who commit no crime if they can seize their plunder with adroitness.[8] It did not matter to Barber where he found the truth so long as he conveyed that truth to his readers.

In 1831 John Warner Barber wrote, illustrated and published a book which brought him considerable success and led five years later to the *Connecticut Historical Collections*. The book was *History and Antiquities of New Haven* and in this publication all of Barber's notions about the method and purpose of local history are set forth. His goal was not a "finished production" but a book which would include those subjects thought to be trivial by those "who write regular histories." As a compiler he was drawn to traditions and interesting anecdotes and even to such legends as the story of the ship that New Haveners thought they saw in the sky in 1647. The book has no apparent organization, is inaccurate in a number of factual points, and suffers with its extensive quotes from excessive padding. Part Chamber of Commerce guidebook, the book praised New Haven and Yale College for providing the best place in all of the United States for acquiring a literary education. For all its faults, it still ranks as one of the earliest local histories in Connecticut and certainly the first that fea-

8. John Warner Barber, *An Account of the Most Important and Interesting Religious Events* (New Haven: 1833), iii–iv.

tures numerous illustrations both of copper plate engravings and wood engravings.

A sound businessman who abhorred waste, Barber throughout his working life found ways again and again to reuse engravings from previous publications. The six plates that were engraved in 1825 for *Views of New Haven* were incorporated into his history of New Haven. The same plates, much worn, were still being pressed into service for a pamphlet by Charles Townshend on the "Invasion of New Haven" published in 1879. Towards the end of his life, Barber eked out a small income by renting the blocks that he had used in the *Connecticut Historical Collections* and in other state volumes. Only when his publications went into successive editions was Barber able to make a reasonable profit from his initial labor.

In the course of preparing illustrations for the history of New Haven, Barber went beyond the confines of the city and began taking views of towns within the bounds of the old New Haven Colony. Beinecke Library has pen and ink drawings of Milford and Orange taken in 1831 but not used in the book. In 1832 there was sufficient demand for copies of the New Haven history to warrant a second edition, this time issued with a re-engraving of Amos Doolittle's "Battle of Lexington," on which Amos Doolittle worked, the last thing he worked on before his death that year.

Sometime over the next two years Barber formed plans to develop an illustrated history of Connecticut featuring views of every town. In 1834 he purchased a horse and buggy from Mr. Daggett for $110 and for three years between the months of April and November he toured the state making pencil drawings of the various towns and cities of Connecticut. He often travelled with friends who appear in so many of the views and stayed overnight in one town or another. When he returned home and through the winter months Barber would take the pencil drawings and develop ink wash drawings. Then he prepared his engraved blocks.

Barber was not sure how to title this publication. His diary first refers to an "historical cabinet." Several months later he mentions his "History of Connecticut," then his "History and Antiquities of Connecticut." Finally, in May of 1836 Barber notes in his diary that he was examining proof for the "Con. Hist. Coll."

Work continued up to the last minute. Barber finished the

to the book. That response indicated a fairly healthy sale, but Barber was not entirely pleased with his agents. In June he wrote to one individual in Stonington assuring his correspondent that the work would be out in September and that it would exceed the description in the prospectus. Barber indicated that his agent in Middletown had gotten 50 or 60 names, but that he was a young man with no experience. According to Barber, the agent had made little effort and had collected no names in the town of Chatham.[12] An examination of the subscription list appended to the first edition of the *Collections* indicates that many towns in the state were not approached before publication.

Within two years John Warner Barber and Asaph Willard sold 6,000 copies of *The Connecticut Historical Collections*. By any standards that was a remarkable sale. Furthermore the demand kept up. A second edition was brought out in 1837, another in 1838, and others in 1846, 1849, 1856 and 1857. No accurate figures have been developed for total sales of the popular history, but it may total as many as 20,000 copies.

Review copies of the book were sent to the editors of newspapers in Danbury and New Haven. Complimentary copies were given to Noah Webster, Abner Reed, Frederick Butler, Edward C. Herrick and Professor Benjamin Silliman. A few notices, all relatively favorable, appeared in the press. A monthly magazine published in the Elm City, The *New Havener*, praised the book in exactly the terms Barber might have wished. "The compiler personally visited every quarter of the state, and collected facts connected with the early history of the several towns, together with a mass of local anecdotes, which would be overlooked by the general historian, as unimportant—but which, in fact, form the most interesting and useful portion of our history." The notice suggested that the book should be acquired by every family in the state. The only criticism made by the New Haven *Palladium*, a newspaper then less than 10 years old, was that Barber had not mentioned the *Palladium* by name. It too declared the book "ought to be possessed by everyman who claims Connecticut as his place of birth." The editors of the *Northern Courier* and the *Daily Herald* both praised Barber for exceeding the terms outlined in the prospectus. The best description of the impact of *Connecticut Historical Collections* was given by Henry Howe, the

12. Barber, Account Book 2, Beinecke Library.

son of a New Haven printer who became a partner of Barber's. According to Howe,

> the book came upon the people like a work of magic. Few had ever seen pictures of places with which they were acquainted. But here was a book that showed multitudes the very houses in which they were born, the school-houses where they had been taught, the churches where they had worshiped God, and the hills where from infancy they had seen the sun set every night in his sublime circuit around our globe. Every village and town was shown, birth places and monuments of noted men, historical localities, and so on. Every man in Connecticut, after he got that book and saw what a grand little state she was, how glorious her history, furnishing as she did more soldiers, more food, and more general supplies to the Revolutionary army, in proportion to population, than any other, felt at least two inches taller. Never had any book been published on any State that so fed the fires of patriotism as did that of the people of Connecticut.[13]

Barber's career continued for nearly fifty years until his death in 1885. He went on to write and illustrate scores of books achieving a modest, local fame and financial self-sufficiency but never wealth. Beginning with the Massachusetts volume in which he commissioned other engravers to work from sketches which he took, Barber compiled other state volumes modeled after *Connecticut Historical Collections.* A simple man of great integrity and industry, Barber deserves recognition as a popularizer of history and a careful and competent illustrator.

CPB

13. Joseph P. Smith, "Henry Howe, the Historian," *Ohio Archeological and Historical Publications*, IV, 1895, 317.

“DRAWINGS TAKEN ON THE SPOT”

TO ONE TURNING the pages of John Warner Barber's *Connecticut Historical Collections*, the book, except for its woodcuts, might seem at first much like other gazetteers. As in Pease and Nile's 1819 *Connecticut and Rhode Island*, Barber's entries for each town give the usual statistics: population, area, date of founding, personages of note, principal industries, important buildings, local sites of interest. But if one turns from such matters-of-fact to Barber's preface, one can be in for a surprise: the author suggests transcendent aims for his book:

> The power by which we recall past scenes, the rapidity with which they are brought in view before us, the faculty by which we can “range o'er creation,” and dwell upon the past and future, demonstrates that man was indeed formed in the image of his Creator, and destined for immortality. By the contemplation of the past, we feel our span of existence extended: we enter into the thoughts, hopes, and aspirations of generations before us, and in such moments hold communion with the departed spirits of antiquity.

Ordinary gazetteers do not “range o'er creation,” or remind us that we are “destined for immortality,” or give promise of extending our “span of existence.” Matters of this sort are more to be expected from a Rousseau or an Emerson or perhaps a Wordsworth. But in Barber's *Connecticut Historical Collections* high matters are addressed that have occupied “men of the greatest intellect the world ever produced.” Such intellects, Barber found, are able to evolve large truths out of the minutiae of daily reality. He cites the examples of Samuel Johnson and Sir Matthew Hale: Johnson, who built a great dictionary upon the minutiae of individual words, at the same time employing those very words to convey large truths in splendid contemplative essays; and Sir Matthew Hale, who in his *History of the Common Law of England* established the grand principles of justice on the minutiae of court cases.

Barber did not claim a place for himself beside these great intellects, but he did see himself seeking to extend our awareness by detailing what he found around him in Connecticut. He shared with his contemporaries an eagerness to discover the grand in the particular. Emerson was preaching that “The inevitable mark of wisdom is to see the miraculous in the common"; and Thomas Cole was pleased to find that "The finest scene in the world, one most fitted to awaken sensations of the sublime, is made up of minutest parts." For Barber, the details of every town in Connecticut show not only that Connecticut "is second to none of her sister states in the virtue, genius, and enterprize of her sons" but demonstrate that "man was indeed formed in the image of his Creator, and destined for immortality."

The attitude toward the good life that Barber displays in his text and pictures had its roots in the eighteenth and early nineteenth centuries. The United States was a new nation, and Barber, publishing *Connecticut Historical Collections* in 1836, displayed his pride in his country. Liberty caps appear prominently in several of his townscapes: Brookfield, Cheshire, and Danbury, the latter featuring both a liberty cap and an eagle. But in addition to this manifest patriotism, his interest in little towns and villages—not just in centers of commerce—reflects a public sensibility strongly developed, first in England and a little later in America, in the second half of the eighteenth century, a sensibility that helped shape the romantic movement of the nineteenth. Barber's eagerness to picture these places and to make the engravings easily available to a wide audience also stems from developments on both sides of the Atlantic in art, journalism, and literature.

Barber's basic method in *Connecticut Historical Collections* was to provide for each town a few paragraphs of statistical and descriptive material accompanied by one or more woodcuts, the whole made conveniently available to the general public in book form. It was a kind of presentation not unknown on either side of the Atlantic, having been made familiar in England in the widely circulated *Gentleman's Magazine*, the popularity of which is attested to by the large number of bound annual volumes still to be found in many collections. This magazine, which began publication in London in 1731, is usually credited with being the world's first general circulation magazine. Over many years its editors gradually developed a picture-and-text formula for introducing urban readers to provincial villages and towns. The formula took a long time to develop. The magazine had been publishing for nine years before it ran any "view": it was a "View of the Town and Castle of St. Augustine in Florida, and the English camp before it." It took forty years more before the magazine routinely gave its readers glimpses of the many charming picturesque villages and towns that scatter the English countryside. By no means was the publication of engravings of townscapes and villagescapes the self-evident sort of feature it seems today—either in England or America. We learn from Linton's *History of Wood-Engraving in America* (1882) that prior to the early 1840s American magazines found little use for wood-engravings "beyond illustrating some new invention, some improvement in the thousand and one articles of household use, or farming utensils, or machinery; or in counterfeiting foreign labels for perfumery. . . ."

There are good reasons why publishers on both sides of the water were slow to carry stories and pictures about the charming villages which are today among the chief attractions for tourists—and why readers were slow to demand information about such places. In England small provincial settlements were of little consequence to city dwellers until the march of commerce made it inescapably evident that provincial industry was vital to the economic wellbeing of London and other large centers. By that time the nation's road system, spurred by commerce, had developed to the point where travel was less hazardous and less uncomfortable than it had been earlier in the eighteenth century. In America, interest in the hinterland followed much the same pattern of development: it burgeoned as transportation became easier. G. M. Davison's *The Traveller's Guide*, which came out the year before Barber's book on Connecticut, noted that "the increased facilities for travelling [including railroads and canals], have greatly augmented the number of tourists within a short period."

In the late eighteenth and early nineteenth centuries, both in England and in America, small-town life began to seem simpler, purer, less hectic than the life that cities offer, and popular writers began to celebrate the beneficence of the village environment. As early as 1751 Thomas Gray observed that country folk live "far from the madding crowd's ignoble strife." In 1770 Oliver Goldsmith, writing of his native Auburn, called it "the loveliest village of the plain / Where health and plenty cheered the laboring swain," a setting "Where humble happiness endeared each scene." In America, Washington Irving early in the next century celebrated the honest, stalwart life of our Sleepy Hollows and of such rural spots as

Rip Van Winkle's village at the foot of the Katskills. For Longfellow, the village blacksmith under his spreading chestnut tree was a figure of heroic cast. The benign view of small-town life gave credence to the patriotic thought that the towns and villages of a state like Connecticut could produce the sort of men who, to use Barber's words, "were the men to whom the world owes the preservation of civil and religious liberty." Barber's own home town of East Windsor provided a case in point, for it was the birthplace of Jonathan Edwards who, Barber says, was considered "the greatest of modern divines."

In the visual arts, the increasingly benign view of small-town life nourished a demand for prints showing rural scenes and country villages. The era of the picturesque had dawned, "picturesque" being popularly applied in its literal sense of "like a picture." In England, a leading proponent of the picturesque was William Gilpin, whose volumes of *Picturesque Tours* became the principal guidebooks for travelers in the late 1700s and early 1800s. Gilpin told travelers not only where the best scenes were to be found but just where to stand and in what direction to face so that the views would fall into the most correct compositions with the right proportions of sky and foreground, the right diagonals, and the right contrasts of texture and color. The search for the picturesque became something of a craze. Travelers were advised to regard landscape with the aesthetic eye of a Nicholas Poussin or Claude Lorrain. To help them do this, the most ardent travelers used what came to be called "Claude glasses," yellowed mirrors in which to view landscapes. The traveler would turn away from the natural scene and view the landscape in the mirror, framing and composing it as if it were a painting, the yellowed glass giving the impression of old varnish, as on a landscape by Claude himself. According to Linton, "the imitation of current English works, to say nothing of the influence of English engravers . . . could not but affect the character of American art," and the American landscape soon found picturesque admirers. As early as 1815 the visiting Russian artist Paul Svinin published a *Picturesque Voyage to North America.* Books on the picturesque usually had much to say about the framing of scenes, the distribution of masses, shapes, forms, and atmospheric effects. Barber's comments on the Housatonic Falls at Canaan are in the tradition: "Here, in a formidable mass on the western side, and on the eastern, the water rushes from the rapid torrent above, and descending in every variety of form, with the mass of foam at the bottom rising in a misty cloud, and the surrounding scenery presents a scene of remarkably picturesque beauty." By 1839 tourists to Cambridge, Massachusetts could while away an afternoon at the local cemetery with their *Picturesque Pocket Companion and Visitor's Guide through Mount Auburn.*

With this kind of intellectual and aesthetic background, Barber visited each Connecticut town in a one-horse wagon to seek information from local antiquarians and to select sites that would give readers an accurate picture of each place. While at the town he took the first of three steps in the production of the illustrations for his books: he made an on-the-spot pencil sketch measuring about 2½″ x 4″. On his sketches he noted the place and the direction from which each scene was viewed, adding further notes on the kinds of trees and anything else he wished to remember. Sometimes he made marginal drawings giving details of a house or other object of interest. These pencil drawings and notes served as the basis for the second step, the preparing of ink washes that he would after convert to engravings. It is these ink washes that are illustrated in the following pages. Barber's final step was to engrave wood blocks, guided by his ink washes. The illustrations in his *Connecticut Historical Collections* were printed from these woodblocks.

The sequence from pencil sketch to ink wash to woodcut is well illustrated in the evolution of Barber's rendering of Glastonbury's cotton factory village. The first step, the pencil sketch (Fig. 1), gives contours of the land, the shapes of the houses and trees, and other prominent features of the scene. Trees are little more than sticks. A penciled note at the bottom of the sketch identifies the location and view. A note at the left reads "buttonwood interspersed with hemlock," and at the right "hemlock." In the top margin Barber notes "Falls 50′ dam. . . ."

In the next step, the pencil sketch is converted into an ink wash (Fig. 2), which now shows hemlocks at the right interspersed with leafy trees (presumably buttonwood), and hemlocks at the left. Sky and water have gradations of shading, and the water reflects the nearby buildings and part of the riverbank. Human figures have been added. A man at the far left—a viewer within the scene, a favorite type in Barber's

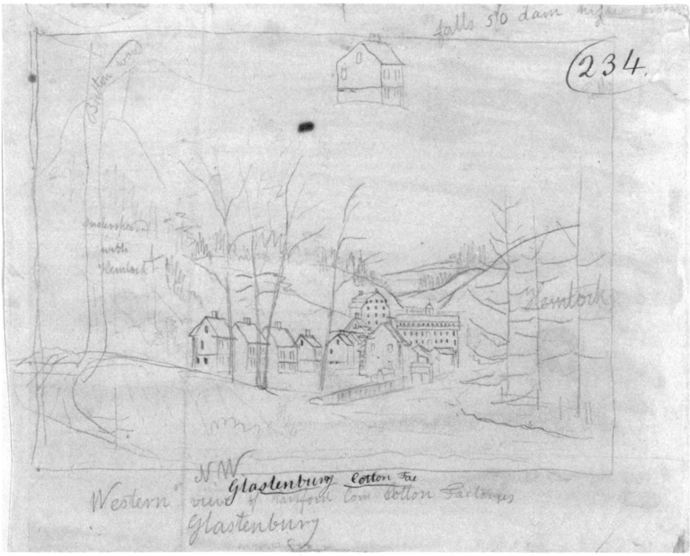

Fig. 1

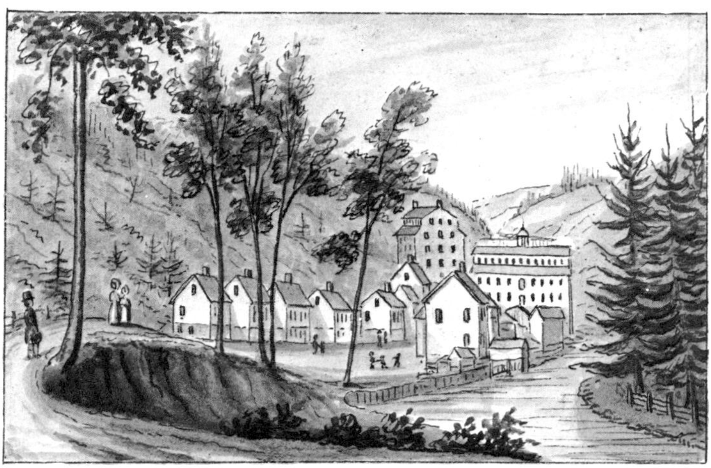

Fig. 2

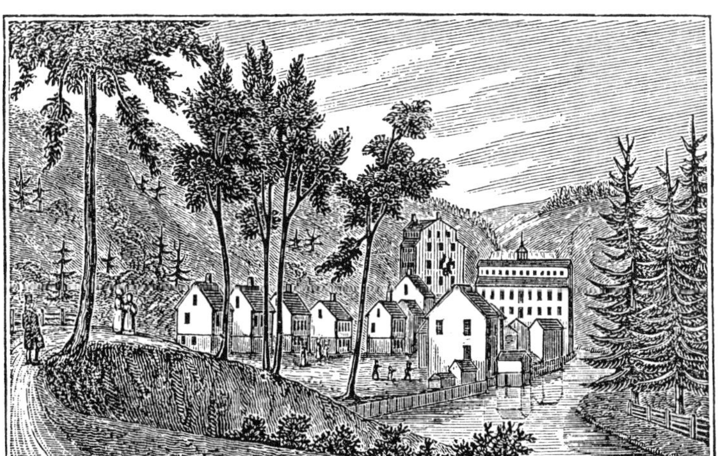

Fig. 3

illustrations—gazes at the distant buildings. A little further to the right two women in bonnets stand chatting. In the village an adult and a child watch as three children play.

In the third step the Glastonbury scene becomes a woodcut (Fig. 3). The new medium gives a new effect. The subtle shading of the sky in the ink wash now gives way to the crisper cuts of the chisel, the reflections in the water become more strictly linear, and the road and embankment at the lower left take on a more uniform texture than is shown in the wash. For the text to accompany this engraving of Glastonbury, Barber turned to Gideon Welles, who would one day be named Secretary of the Navy under Abraham Lincoln. Welles' response to Barber's request for information is preserved in the archives of The Connecticut Historical Society.

Despite variations resulting from the translations of the scenes from one medium to another, Barber insisted on the accuracy of his renderings. In the Preface to *Connecticut Historical Collections* he wrote:

> The numerous engravings interspersed through this work, were (with five or six exceptions) executed from drawings taken on the spot, by the author of this work. Before deciding upon the correctness of these representations, he wishes his readers to consider, that the appearance of any place will vary considerably as it is viewed from different points: thus, a *north* view will appear quite different from one taken at the *south*. A person not being used to see a place from the point from which the drawing is taken, it may not at first sight be readily recognized. Before any view is condemned as being incorrect, it will be necessary, in order to form a correct judgment, to stand on the place from whence the drawing was made.

The members of the Acorn Club responsible for the picture captions in the following pages have accepted Barber's challenge and have visited each scene, standing, where possible, on the spot chosen by the artist.

Barber was well aware that readers might suspect him of sacrificing accuracy for aesthetic effect; in minor matters he clearly does so. For example, he shows houses reflected in Glastonbury's Roaring Brook, as if in a still pond, whereas the stream's rapid eddies rarely if ever reflect their surroundings. Still, there is no need to doubt the essential accuracy of Barber's renderings. In his Preface to *Historical Collections of the State of New York*, published three years after his Connecticut book, he insisted that his "principal object was to give faithful representations, rather than picturesque views, or beautiful specimens of art," and he again urged skeptical readers to go to the very locations to see for themselves. Nevertheless, there can be little doubt about his picturesque interest. Again and again he shows an artist (perhaps himself) sketching[1]. He further emphasizes picturesque interest by introducing figures who point out, often to a companion, some feature of the view, as if to say, "Just look at this scene!"[2] Again Barber's aesthetic sensibility is evident where he shows adult couples, or parents and children, sharing the pleasures of a stroll along the pictured pathways.[3]

The aesthete in Barber did not always rest completely at ease with the faithful reporter in him. The reporter often won, with the pictorial consequence that in many of his pictures he places the observer in the middle of the road, precisely where a reader of his book might find himself in approaching the town. Accurate though this arrangement may be, a pictorial disadvantage is that the road itself can split the composition down the middle.[4] Again, in the interests of verisimilitude, Barber tends to present his views from normal eye level. He has no bird's eye views like those that later became a feature of O. H. Bailey's townscapes. One consequence of this eye-level viewpoint is that the scene can fall into a series of horizontal layers, as in the view of Danbury (Page 23). In the Danbury picture a low foreground, which the viewer seems to share with two figures who also view the town, lies parallel to the bottom margin. Above this foreground lies a middle ground, its horizontality emphasized by straight fence lines dividing the fields. The next layer above that shows the houses of the village stretching across the picture from border to border. Above these, a row of low hills forms a fourth layer. The sky comprises the fifth and top layer. Others of his horizontally

1. For example in Collinsville, Farmington, Granby, Montville, and Stamford, among others.

2. For example in Canterbury, Hamden, Madison, Norfolk, Norwalk, Saybrook, and others.

3. For example in Branford, Canterbury, Colchester, Danbury, Durham, Plymouth, Thompson, and others.

4. For example, in Brookfield, Bloomfield, Hamden, and others.

composed townscapes sometimes omit the middle ground or the layer of hills.[5]

In his most successful compositions Barber breaks the grip of layered horizontality. For example, in the view of Tariffville (Page 86) the foreground, which at either side rises about a quarter of the way up the picture, dips in the middle down to the lower border, where a sketcher sits with a companion. A group of buildings, about half way up the picture plane at the left, swings down and forward at the right, spilling into the middleground. Behind the buildings, wooded hills at the right give way to distant countryside at the left. A tall evergreen occupies most of the left side of the picture, adding importantly to the depth of the view, as can be easily demonstrated by blocking it out. In another scene, Westport (Page 103), Barber successfully modifies the strong horizontality of the design with the diagonal of the road and with a second diagonal extending from the church on the hill down through a series of buildings to the bridge and then to the fence at the lower right. The two buildings in the foreground at either side frame the composition and add to its apparent depth.

If correctness was a major concern in Barber's illustrations, it was by no means the only concern. In the Glastonbury scene, as in many of his other views, the goodness of life in Connecticut is set before us. Though the waters of the aptly named Roaring Brook are shown plunging over their fifty foot dam to turn the wheels of South Glastonbury's major manufactory, the rigors of the industrial revolution are nowhere suggested. Here is the good life a democratic America offers. Children play in the street; women, friendly neighbors with plenty of time on their hands, stop to have a quiet chat; a man, manifestly of aesthetic sensibilities, pauses to gaze at the scene. The viewpoint chosen by the artist is at the side of the country road leading to the village, or perhaps in the middle of the road—just the spot a traveler in search of rural pleasures would select to pause for a moment to reflect on the gentle picturesque beauty of the scene.

Linton, in his *History* comes down pretty hard on Barber as an engraver, remarking that "His chief ambition has been, not success in engraving, but to 'preach the Gospel by means of pictures,' toward which end he has issued, in addition to his

5. For example Madison, Norwalk, Farmington, and others.

historical, various emblematic books." Of Barber's later work Linton observes that "the pious intention asks more praise than either the designs or the engravings." To the extent that this criticism is fair, it serves to justify the present collection of Barber's ink washes, for these washes, here published for the first time, have a charm and nuance heretofore virtually unknown except to a lucky few.

JBM

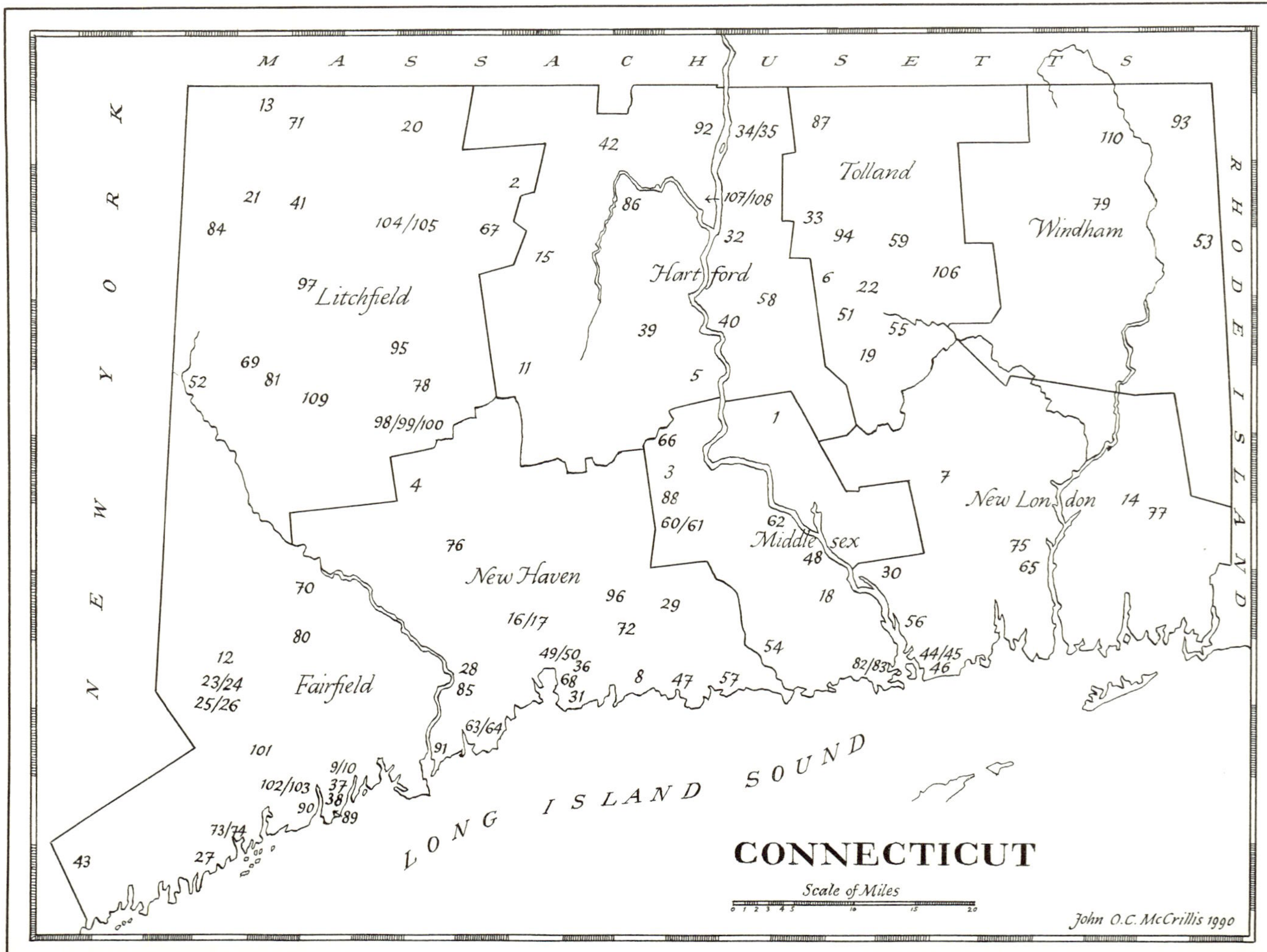

M A S S A C H U S E T T S
N E W Y O R K
R H O D E I S L A N D
Litchfield
Hartford
Tolland
Windham
New London
Middlesex
New Haven
Fairfield
LONG ISLAND SOUND
CONNECTICUT
Scale of Miles
0 1 2 3 4 5 10 15 20
John O.C. McCrillis 1990
13
71
20
42
92
34/35
87
110
93
2
21
41
84
104/105
67
86
107/108
32
33
94
59
79
53
15
97
6
22
106
58
51
40
39
55
95
69
81
109
52
78
11
5
19
98/99/100
1
66
3
88
60/61
62
48
7
14
77
4
76
75
65
30
18
70
96
29
16/17
72
56
80
54
12
49/50
36
68
31
8
47
57
82/83
44/45
46
28
85
23/24
25/26
63/64
91
101
9/10
102/103
37
38
89
90
73/74
27
43

1. Ashford
2. Barkhamsted
3. Berlin
4. Bethlehem
5. Bloomfield
6. Bolton
7. Bozrah
8. Branford
9. Bridgeport
10. Bridgeport
11. Bristol
12. Brookfield
13. Canaan
14. Canterbury
15. Canton
16. Cheshire
17. Cheshire
18. Chester
19. Colchester
20. Colebrook
21. Cornwall
22. Coventry
23. Danbury
24. Danbury
25. Danbury
26. Danbury
27. Darien
28. Derby
29. Durham
30. East Haddam
31. East Haven
32. East Windsor
33. Ellington
34. Enfield
35. Enfield
36. Fair Haven
37. Fairfield
38. Fairfield
39. Farmington
40. Glastonbury
41. Goshen
42. Granby
43. Greenwich
44. Groton
45. Groton
46. Groton
47. Guilford
48. Haddam
49. Hamden
50. Hamden
51. Hebron
52. Kent
53. Killingly
54. Killingworth
55. Lebanon
56. Lyme
57. Madison
58. Manchester
59. Mansfield
60. Meriden
61. Meriden
62. Middletown
63. Milford
64. Milford
65. Montville
66. New Britain
67. New Hartford
68. New Haven
69. New Milford
70. Newtown
71. Norfolk
72. North Haven
73. Norwalk
74. Norwalk
75. Norwich
76. Oxford
77. Plainfield
78. Plymouth
79. Pomfret
80. Redding
81. Roxbury
82. Saybrook
83. Saybrook
84. Sharon
85. Shelton
86. Simsbury
87. Somers
88. Southington
89. Southport
90. Stamford
91. Stratford
92. Suffield
93. Thompson
94. Tolland
95. Torrington
96. Wallingford
97. Warren
98. Watertown
99. Watertown
100. Watertown
101. Weston
102. Westport
103. Westport
104. Winchester
105. Winchester
106. Windham
107. Windsor
108. Windsor
109. Woodbury
110. Woodstock

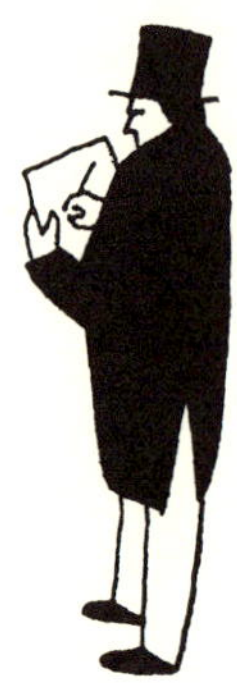

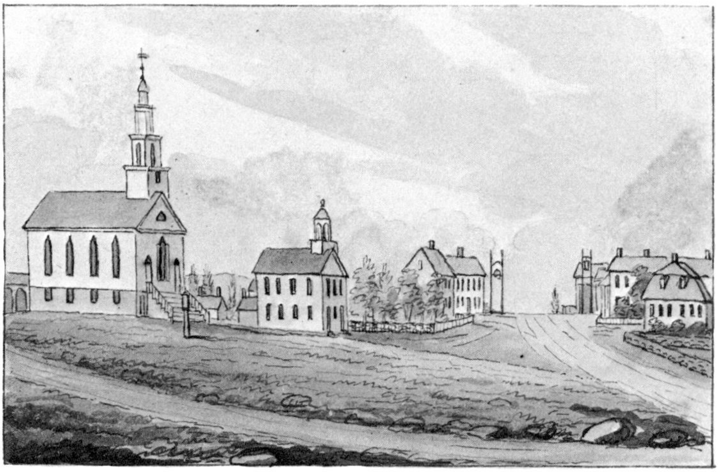

ASHFORD

SOUTHWESTERN VIEW OF ASHFORD

"No town has suffered so severely from modern 1
changes as Ashford," wrote Ellen Larned in 1880. The prosperous town center of Ashford with its new Congregational church erected in 1830, its academy, and its hotels, fell into a slow decline in the years after Barber took his view. Ashford was one of those Windham County towns completely bypassed by the railroad. A modern traveler driving along Route 44 may notice the surviving academy building constructed in the late 1820s and now undergoing restoration so that it can serve as a local museum, but all of the other structures in Barber's ink wash, including the two hotels and the First Congregational Church, have disappeared.

CPB

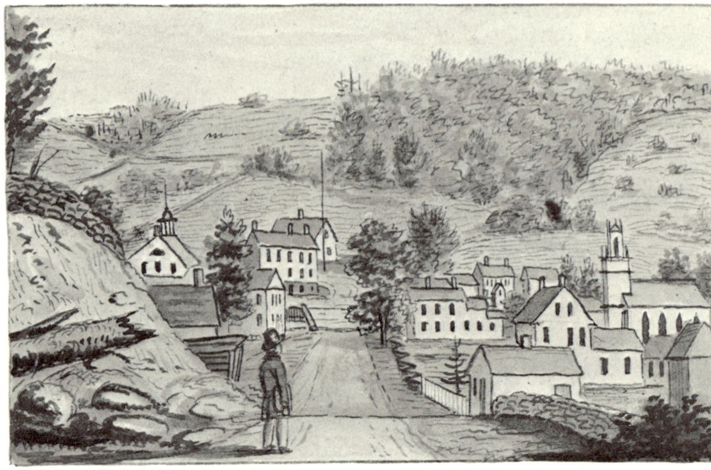

BARKHAMSTED

WEST VIEW OF HITCHCOCKSVILLE

2 HITCHCOCKSVILLE IN BARKHAMSTED looks today much as it did in Barber's time. The slope at the left is still an open lot and the house at the right still stands, though nothing remains of its barn (the nearest building on the right) but its foundation stones. The chair factory Barber mentions is the Hitchcock Factory building at the left, with the cupola which is still a feature of its roofline. The building directly across the bridge at the foot of the road over the west branch of the Farmington River is now the Riverton Inn. Above the door of the church at the right appears the carved inscription "Union Church, founded July 4, 1829." It was an Episcopal church, which now houses the Hitchcock Museum, displaying chairs and other furniture related to the famous furniture-maker's designs. A red brick house, in the picture just above the viewer's head, still stands, among some more recent additions on that side of the street, including a bracketed 19th-century Italianate building, now a general store. The best way to reach the point where the viewer in the picture is standing is to take the Riverton road off Connecticut Route 44 just north of New Hartford.

JBM

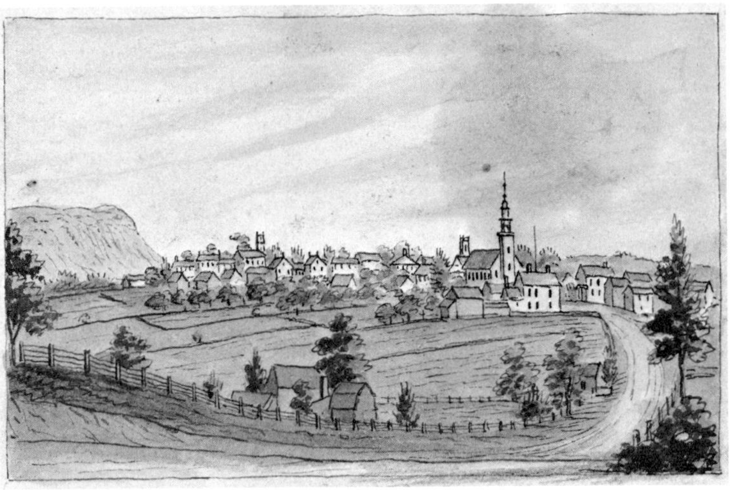

BERLIN

NORTHERN VIEW OF WORTHINGTON

BARBER'S VIEW OF THE BOROUGH of Worthington in the 3
town of Berlin was taken from the north looking south with the prominent landmark, Mount Lamentation, rising to the left or the southeast corner. The borough, created in 1834, featured three churches and an academy. Two of the churches can be seen in Barber's view: a Universalist church on the left and the Congregational church on the right. The structure with the four-pronged cupola was an academy built in 1833. The Universalist church, without its cupola, is now a private residence. The Congregational church later served as the town hall and a schoolhouse. The academy building is now serving the town as the home of the Berlin Free Library.

Along Worthington Ridge still stand a number of handsome, late eighteenth and early nineteenth century homes of brick and wood, as well as the old town hall, academy, and fire district. The village achieved fame as the place where the Pattison brothers started the manufacture of tinware in America, from which grew the legend of the Yankee peddler and Connecticut's pejorative nickname, "the Nutmeg State." Worthington is the birthplace of Emma Hart Willard (1787–1850), a pioneer in women's education.

ESG

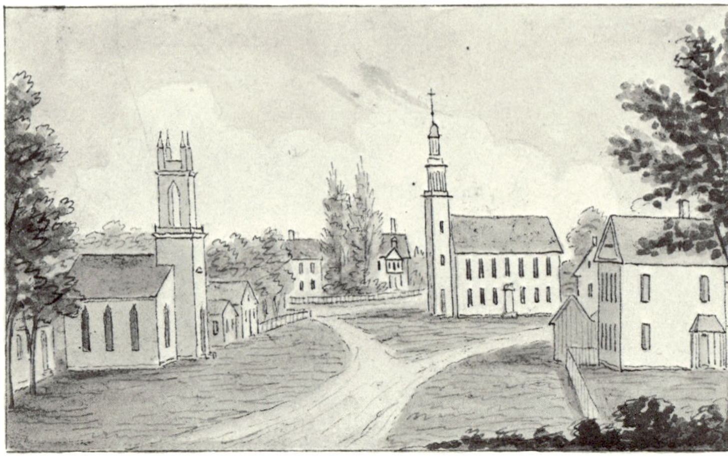

BETHLEHEM

4 THE TWO CHURCHES in Barber's Bethlehem scene stand a few rods south of the junction of state Routes 61 and 132. The Episcopal church on the left looks much as it did when Barber pictured it. It is of locally manufactured red brick in the Gothic Revival style. Diagonally across the street stands the Congregational church—not the building shown by Barber, which was replaced by a new structure in 1836.

Between the two churches and behind the fence Barber shows the Bellamy House at the right and the Backus House at the left. Joseph Bellamy, born in 1719, became one of the most influential men in American religious life in the 18th century. The first pastor of the Congregational church, he conducted in his home what is believed to have been the first theological school in the American colonies.

Azel Backus, born in 1791, became the second pastor of the Congregational church. A graduate of Yale, he received an honorary D.D. from Princeton in 1810, and went on to become the first President of Hamilton College, New York, in 1812.

JBM

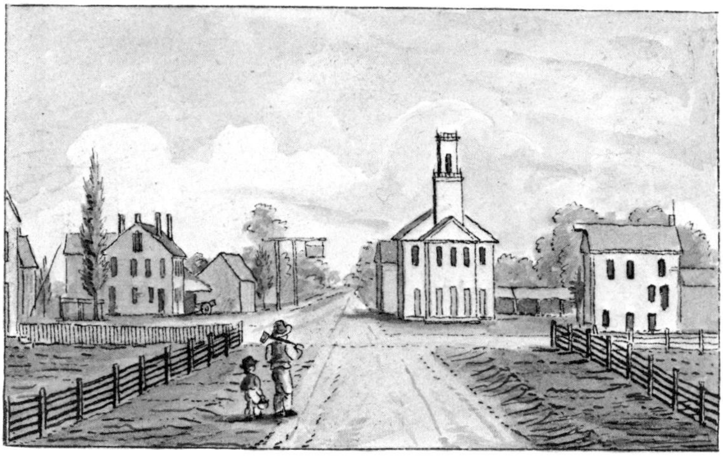

BLOOMFIELD
SOUTH VIEW OF THE
CONGREGATIONAL CHURCH

THE WINTONBURY CHURCH illustrated above was the second church on this location and was built in 1801, replacing the first church built in 1736. The present third church was built in the same place in 1858. Wintonbury Parish became a town named Bloomfield in 1835. The present church is substantially larger and more imposing than Barber's picture of the second church. And in 1957 it was vastly increased in size by a large brick addition given by Philip B. Gales, a resident of Bloomfield and a parishioner. The present church is located at the corner of Tunxis Avenue and Wintonbury Avenue, and faces the attractive village green in the center of Bloomfield to the left. As one faces the village green one sees on the left, or west, the Prosser Library, an outstanding suburban library and on the right Wintonbury Mall, an attractive modest size shopping center.

JMK

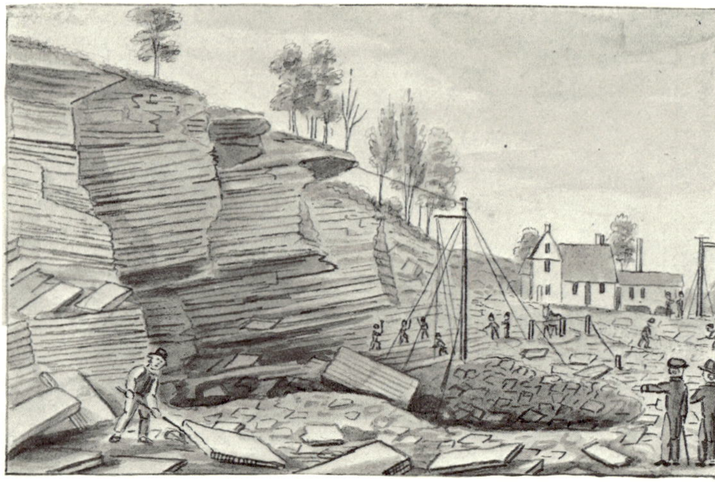

BOLTON

BOLTON STONE QUARRY

6 NEEDLESS TO SAY, the quarry shown in Barber's drawing is still in existence. Now known as the Bolton Notch Quarry, it is still in operation, with a small office building on the site.

To reach the quarry travel by Routes 6 and 44 (same road) or I384 past Manchester to Bolton Notch. Just before the two highway signs at the Notch (left—Route 44 and right—Route 6) turn right onto Notch Road. After crossing over the railroad tracks, the Quarry is on the immediate right, just over a small bridge.

DBE

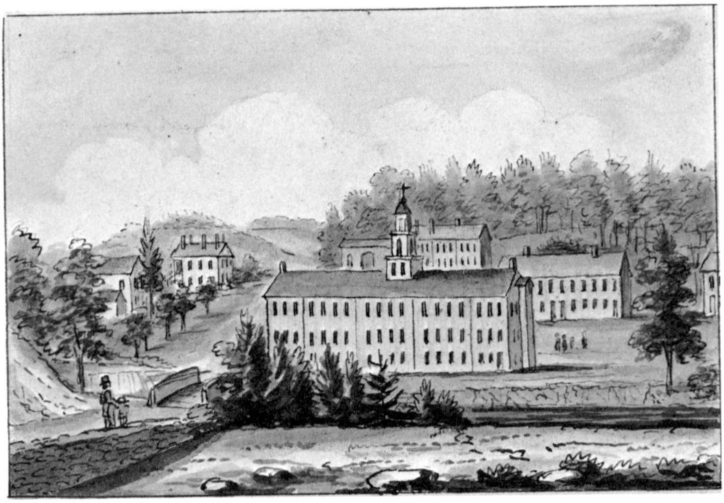

BOZRAH

EAST VIEW OF FITCHVILLE

THE STONE FACTORY shown in Barber's drawing is still 7
standing. It was built in 1814 on the Yantic River to house the Bozrah Manufacturing Company and to produce cotton goods. Fitchville was named for Colonel Asa Fitch (1755–1844), its founder, and in the eighteenth century was the site of an iron works.

Fitchville remains a northeastern part of Bozrah, but at the time of this writing (1989), was about to lose its United States Post Office, in a consolidation with the Bozrah post office.

Fitchville is located on an unnumbered road and can be reached via Route 2 between Colchester and Norwich. East from Colchester take Exit 23. West from Norwich take Exit 24. Barber's viewpoint appears to be on the unnumbered road, looking west.

DBE

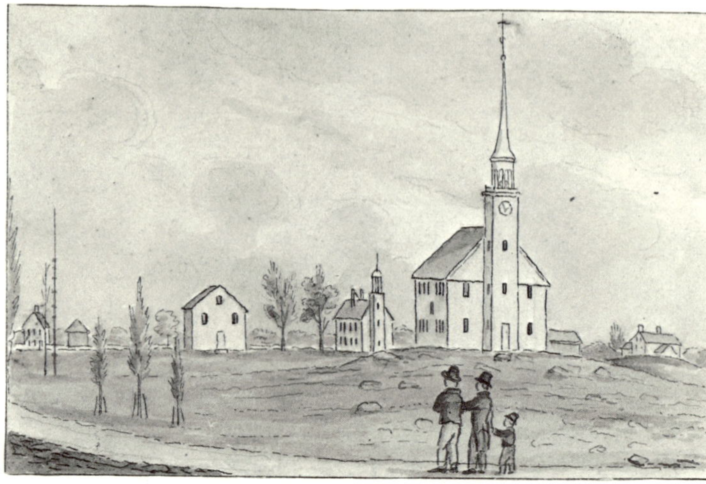

BRANFORD

CENTRAL PART

8 We have here the Branford Green looking from Main Street toward Long Island Sound showing, from left to right, a small Episcopal church with a door and three windows, the Academy, and the Congregational church surmounted by a spire. The only survivor today is the Academy which was built in 1820 and has served a variety of community purposes, and it has been moved a short distance. The present Episcopal church dates from 1851, and ground was broken for the First Congregational church in 1843. Between them now are the Town Hall and Court House and a Civil War monument. This location was in Barber's time the very center of Branford, and it remains the center today. It can be approached from Route I-95 by taking either Exit 54 or Exit 55.

FMS, DFM

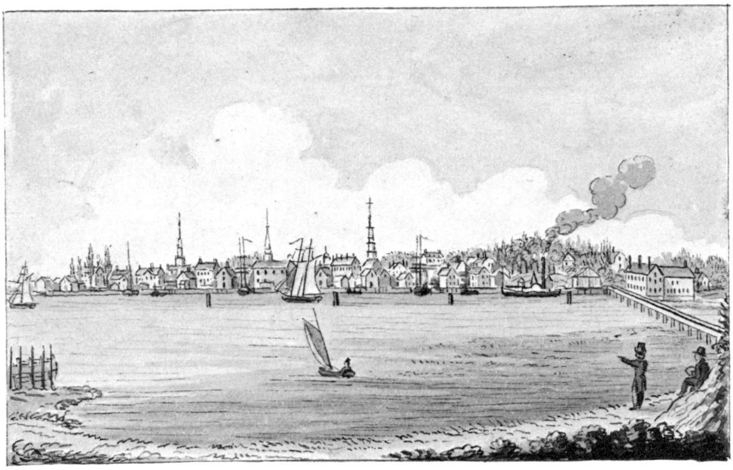

BRIDGEPORT

EASTERN VIEW

THIS SCENE IS DRAWN from a point in East Bridgeport somewhere near the Steel Point Plant of United Illuminating Company, probably in the large fenced-off storage area on East Main Street near Stratford Avenue, perhaps actually underneath the great Connecticut Turnpike overpass. The bridge in this picture crosses the Pequonnock River at a point that might be said to separate the harbor from the river. Barber located it a mile and a half from Long Island Sound. It is probably the one constructed in 1807 to replace the Lottery Bridge, built in 1791, which collapsed in 1804. It connected Stratford Avenue in East Bridgeport with Beaver Street—now Fairfield Avenue—at the site of the present bridge connecting those two streets. Barber would have been standing near the pair of oil tanks in the fenced-off property of U.I., right behind L. Bernstein and Sons' Wholesale Produce at 236 Stratford Avenue.

CC

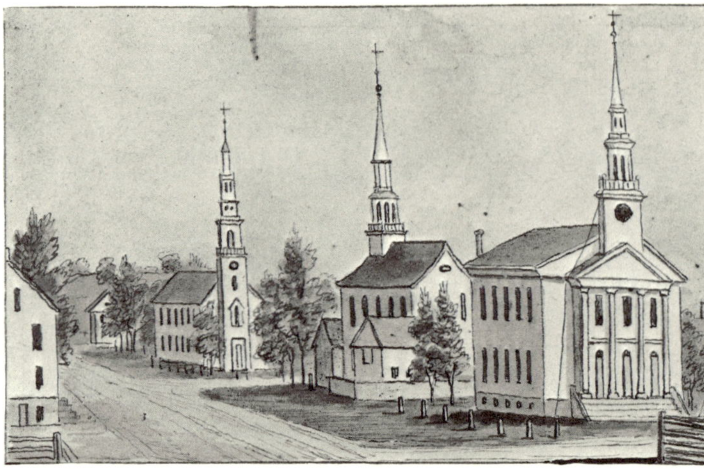

BRIDGEPORT

CHURCHES ON BROAD STREET

10 THESE CHURCHES ON BROAD STREET are, from the nearest to the farthest: the Second Congregational built in 1830; the Baptist, formerly the old Episcopal, built in 1807; the First Congregational built in 1803; the new Episcopal, just being completed as this picture was drawn in 1837; and, mostly concealed, the steepleless Methodist. Barber was looking towards the north. An earlier version of this view (reproduced in David Palmquist's *Bridgeport*) does not include the Episcopal church, a very elegant stone building and the first masonry structure in the city. The churches were on Broad between John and Gilbert streets, the present location of a number of retail stores and office buildings. You can orient yourself by sighting on MeLevy Hall, built in 1853 as the Fairfield County Court House, which stands between what shows here as the second and third steepled churches. Barber was sketching from the west side of Broad Street just south of the present Bridgeport Public Library in the middle of the Hi Ho Center (formerly Lafayette Plaza).

CC

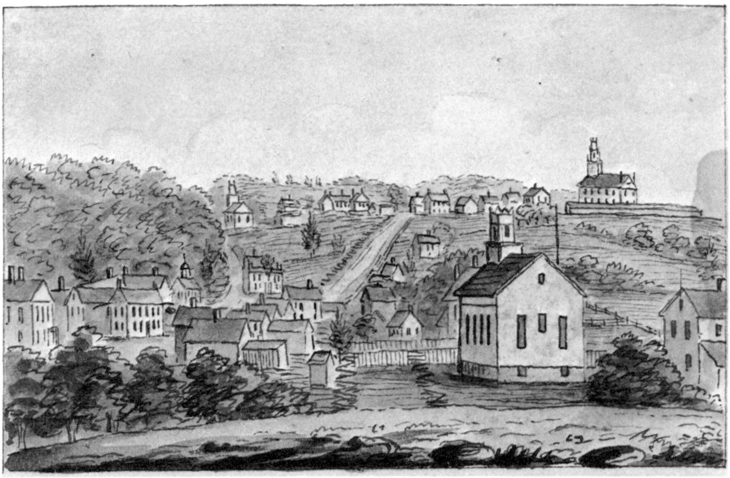

BRISTOL

WESTERN VIEW

John Warner Barber described Bristol as a manufacturing town which could boast no fewer than sixteen clock factories in 1836 producing more than 100,000 clocks annually. His view highlights Bristol's churches, the main thoroughfare leading to Hartford, the East Middle Turnpike, and the portion of the town known as North Village. Several of the buildings in Barber's view were newly constructed when Barber visited, funded, in part, through the profits of industry. The Congregational Church was built in 1832 and the Methodist Church seen in the foreground on the right was constructed in 1835.

A traveler passing through town today on busy Route 6, now a heavily developed commercial strip, will see little of historic interest. The spire of the 1832 Congregational Church is just visible to the present day viewer who positions himself where Barber stood. Surrounding the church on Federal Hill are a number of well preserved nineteenth century buildings, including the home of the American Clock and Watch Museum.

CPB

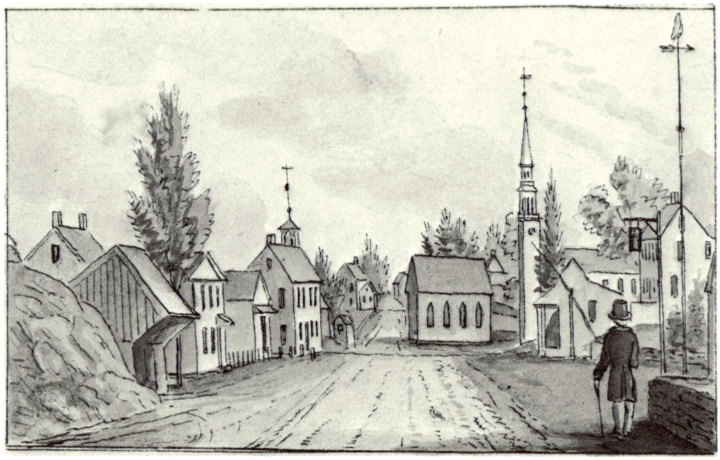

BROOKFIELD

NORTH VIEW

12 JOHN WARNER BARBER took his view of the village of Brookfield on November 5, 1835. He is seen within the view itself looking north at the town center. On the extreme right is a liberty pole, a vestige of the revolutionary period. The three public buildings, from the right, are the Congregational and Episcopal churches and the meeting house with its cupola.

Entering the town center today on Route 25, the essential orientation and some of the buildings from Barber's time remain largely the same. The prominent hill remains to the left. The Episcopal church no longer stands and a Congregational church with a cornerstone dated 1857 has replaced the earlier structure. The town hall has been replaced with a similar building erected around 1875 which is now the home of the local historical society. Three of the five structures in Barber's view on the left hand side have survived.

CPB

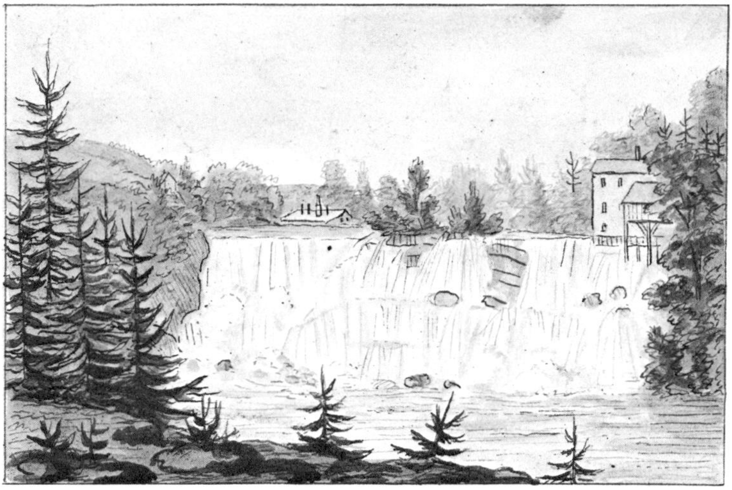

CANAAN

SOUTHWEST VIEW OF THE HOUSATONIC

PICTURES OF WATERFALLS have a hard time of it attempting to convey an impression of the actual experience of a visitor. For one thing, the visitor to the Housatonic Falls shown in Barber's view hears the water, a sound that dominates the ravine and the surrounding banks. Furthermore, the falls change as the volume of water varies from season to season. Barber's picture shows the cataract split into three main sections. At other times the configuration is of a main fall flanked by thin streams. Again, Barber's view suggests water dropping from an almost straight edge down to lower levels and at last to the rapids below. The visitor will find, however, that the curtain of falling water is at different angles at different parts of the drop.

To reach the point from which Barber made his picture one can take Water Street off state Route 126 in Canaan, pass under a trestle bridge, bear right past a riverside power plant, cross over an iron bridge, and then bear right uphill to a view of the falls. From the street, the best view can be had when the leaves are off the trees. There is a footpath through the trees at the edge of the ravine for those who want a clear view in summer.

JBM

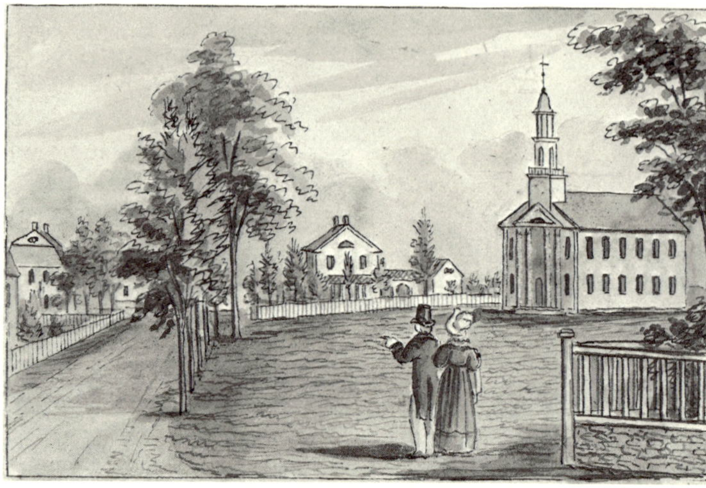

CANTERBURY

SOUTH VIEW

14

The historian-artist positioned himself on the southern corner of the Canterbury town green, looking northward so that he could include both the Prudence Crandall house and the Congregational church in his view. The scene looking across the Canterbury green as it appears today would be recognizable to Barber. The old church, built in the 1790s and burned down in the mid-1960s, has been replaced with a colonial revival structure that unfortunately lacks the distinction of the original. The Prudence Crandall house, now a state museum administered by the Connecticut Historical Commission, still dominates the southwest corner of Routes 169 and 14. A supermarket was built on the site of an old house once owned by Andrew Judson, the man who led the local effort to close the Prudence Crandall school. Directly opposite the Prudence Crandall house stands a largely unchanged federal house. The fenced area shown in the lower right area of Barber's sketch, possibly an animal pound, is no longer there.

CPB

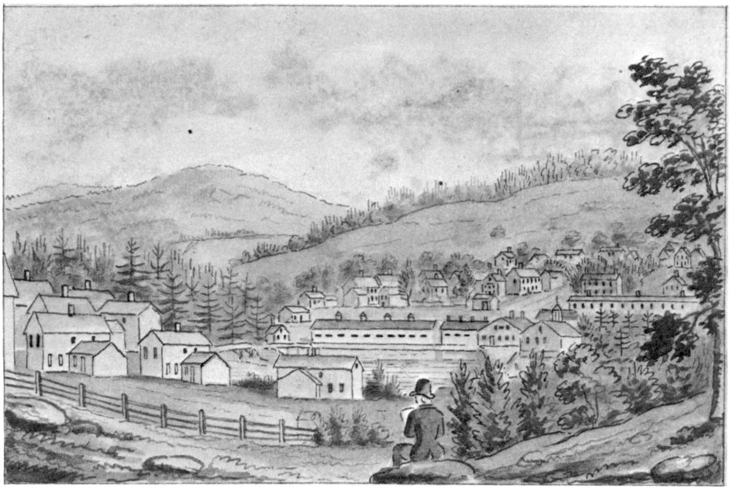

CANTON

WESTERN VIEW OF COLLINSVILLE, IN CANTON

JOHN WARNER BARBER visited the industrial village of Collinsville on October 7, 1834 right in the middle of an economic depression which caused Collins & Company to temporarily close. Founded in 1826 for the manufacture of axes and other edge tools, Collins & Company moved to Canton in 1828 and established its operation on the east side of the Farmington river. In 1831 and 1832 double dwelling houses were constructed on both sides of the river which Barber described, noting the contrast of the white paint with the green foliage, as presenting "a novel and beautiful appearance."

Today's viewer can position himself, as Barber did, above the village looking to the east, but mature trees completely obscure the prospect. Approaching the community on Route 4 from the southeast brings you across the river and past the surviving buildings of Collins & Company. Most of the company houses, which rented for $25 a year in the 1830s, have survived. Shortly after Barber took his view, a Congregational church was constructed which later burned and was replaced in 1858. Collinsville was hard hit by the flood of 1955, but the commercial center, consisting mainly of late nineteenth century structures, has retained much of its original character.

CPB

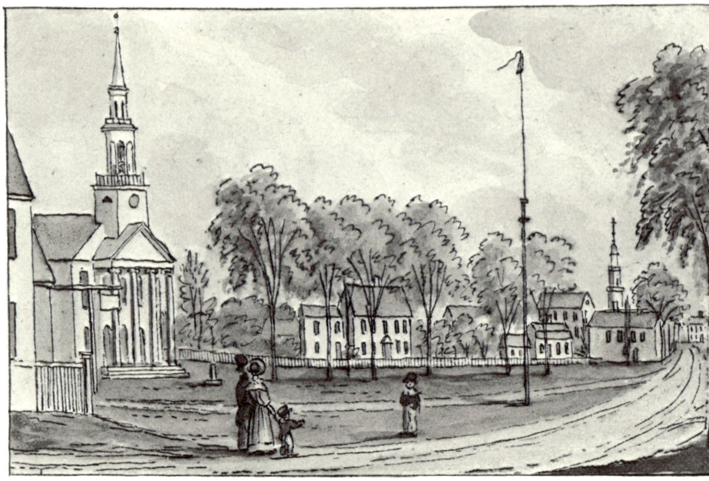

CHESHIRE

SOUTH VIEW (CENTRAL PART)

16 THE FIRST CONGREGATIONAL CHURCH at the left is still standing today, but two other religious edifices seen next to one another toward the right, are gone. The taller one with the steep roof was the Methodist church, and the one with the spire served the Episcopal congregation. The latter has been replaced by the red brick St. Peters' church (Episcopal). To the far right on the opposite side of the street is what was then called the Episcopal Academy and which is now Cheshire Academy. We are looking northwest across Highland Avenue (Route 10) at the intersection of Academy Road (Route 68).

FMS, DFM

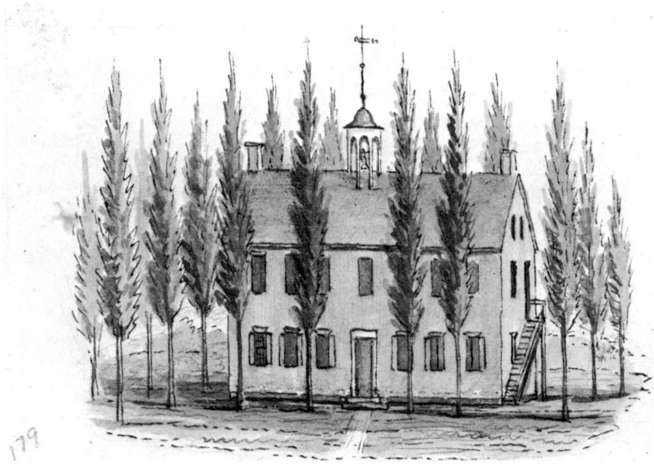

CHESHIRE EPISCOPAL ACADEMY

AT THE TIME the artist made his engraving the Episcopal Academy consisted of this one building, erected the year the school opened in 1796. A substantial brick edifice fifty-four feet by thirty-four, it stood alone on the east side of what is now Highland Avenue (Route 10) just north of Academy Road (Route 68). Later called Horton Hall, it burned down in the very early 1940s. The institution, which has operated continuously since its founding, changed its name to the Roxbury School and finally in 1937 to Cheshire Academy. Today its large campus, filled with many buildings, starts at the intersection of Highland and Academy and spreads north and east for a considerable distance.

FMS, DFM

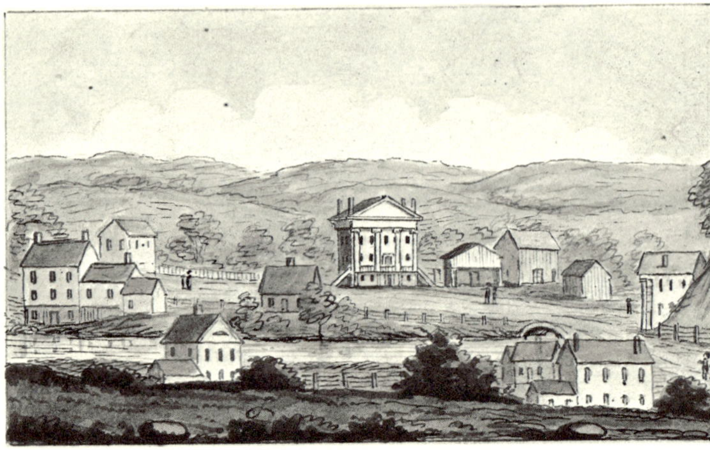

CHESTER

NORTHERN VIEW (CENTRAL PART)

18 BARBER'S VIEW WAS TAKEN from a point a few yards northeast of the present junction of Route 148 and Main Street. Construction has since blocked the view of the Pattaconk River (foreground) and hides most of the buildings beyond it. Coastal trading vessels used to travel up the Pattaconk from the Connecticut River to the cove in the center of this once thriving manufacturing town. The cove is now silted in, though the stream still flows under Main Street at about the point shown by Barber. The four-columned Chester Hotel in the center of the picture has lost its columns, but the columned building at the far right (seen from the side) retains its handsome portico, its second floor serving as the studio of the well-known graphic artist Peter Good. At the far left is the Colt house (late 18th century), whose earliest known owner, Samuel Colt, was partner in a boat yard on the Pattaconk at the foot of his property behind his house.

JBM

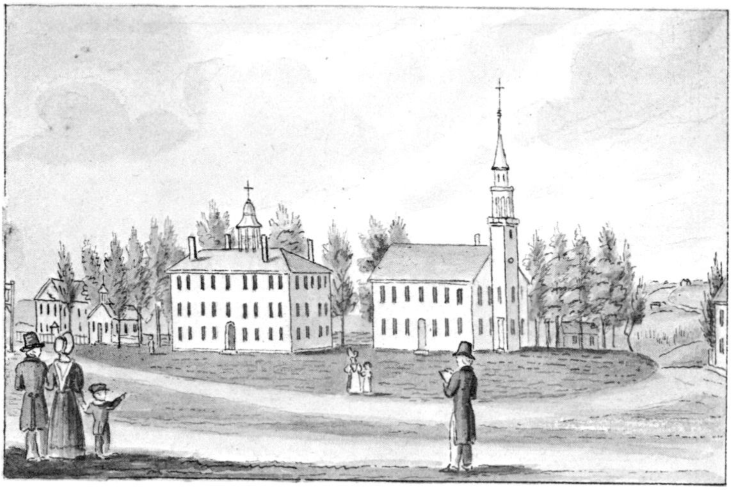

COLCHESTER

BACON ACADEMY AND CONGREGATIONAL CHURCH

THE 1836 VIEW OF COLCHESTER illustrated by John Warner Barber has changed, but not entirely. Bacon Academy's building is still there, but next to it, just to the north is Day Hall, which had formerly been the chapel of the fourth church building of the Congregational meetinghouse, having been built in 1857–58. Day Hall was moved slightly to its present location. It was remodeled and repaired by Edward M. Day a Hartford attorney who had donated most of the money for the fourth church remodeling which made the Colchester Congregational Church a much sounder structure and changed both the exterior of the church from its former Victorian appearance both inside and out, and returned it to its original appearance when it was built in 1841. It had been subjected to two remodelings, in 1885 and again in 1929–30. The present church is located just to the north of Day Hall and faces the Colchester green. Day Hall was presented to Bacon Academy by Mr. Day and is used as the office for the superintendent of schools of Colchester, but the Junior and Senior High Schools are located about half a mile from the village green and are named Bacon Academy.

JMKD

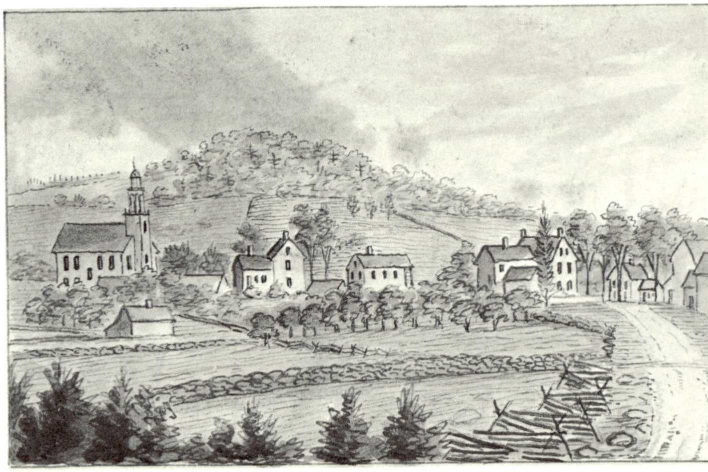

COLEBROOK

SOUTHWESTERN VIEW

THE INDEFATIGABLE BARBER visited Colebrook on October 7, 1835, the same day he traveled to Norfolk and Litchfield. He sketched the town looking northeast, on the main road, leading into the center. On the left of what is now Route 183 is the Federal style Martin Rockwell house, built in 1793, and well preserved today. Further down the road is a building which Barber identifies in his pencil sketch as the post office and which now serves as a general store. In the background is a hilly area called Mount Pisgah. The Congregational church seems to have been placed incorrectly by Barber. The first Congregational church, which was moved from its original location in 1794 as a consequence of a fourteen year struggle between residents, was adjacent to the Martin Rockwell house. It was replaced in 1842 with a Greek Revival church modeled after one in Unionville. Unless further research can resolve this apparent error, this appears to be one of the few examples of inaccuracy in Barber's sketches.

The past is very much alive in this community, the last to be settled in Connecticut. As one local history states: "In Colebrook Center, not much visual change occurs—and for good, is how we residents think of that."

CPB

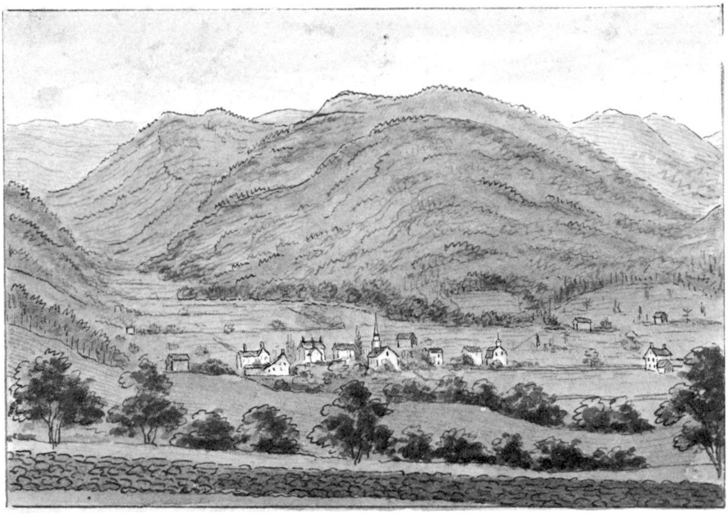

CORNWALL
NORTHEASTERN VIEW OF SOUTH CORNWALL

THE GEORGE WHEATON HOUSE, from which Barber says he took his view of South Cornwall, stands at the corner of what is now Connecticut Route 128 and Town Lane. Barber called the view "one of the most interesting and striking scenes to be met with in the state." It remains a fine view, but it is not quite as Barber shows it, partly on account of the trees that have grown up and partly because of the pattern of ski trails on the hillsides across the valley. What Barber calls South Cornwall was called Cornwall Plain early in the twentieth century; it is now known, to locals at least, as Cornwall Village. The 1938 WPA guide to Connecticut, characterizing a tour from Cornwall Bridge to South Canaan, says "This tour traverses a thoroughly wild and primitive area. Hills, rushing mountain brooks, giant pines and hemlocks, quiet wooded valleys, and little sleepy communities are features of this route." The giant pines, a virgin stand known as the Cathedral Pines, went down on July 10, 1989 in a tornado that cut a wide swath through the town.

JBM

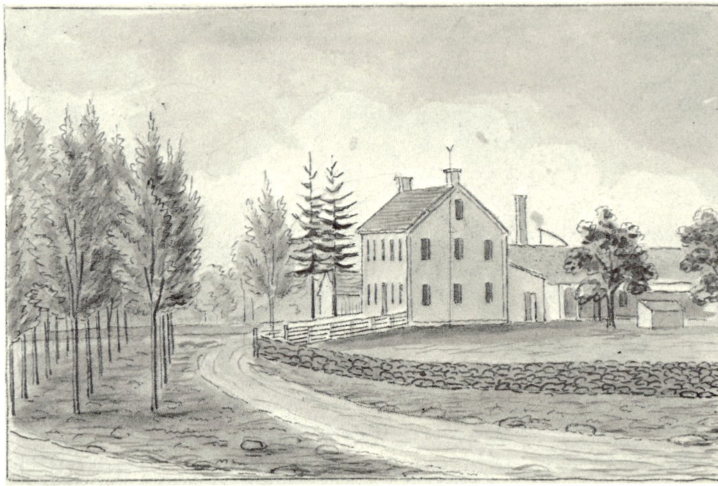

COVENTRY

NORTH VIEW OF THE HALE HOUSE

NATHAN HALE, THE SPY who had but one life to give for his country, emerged as a great American hero in the second quarter of the 19th century. A monument was erected in his honor in Coventry in 1836, dramatic plays were presented and biographies celebrated his life. To represent Coventry, Barber chose to sketch Captain Nathan Hale's birthplace, a fine, central hall house built by Hale's father in 1776. The Hale farm was acquired by antiquarian George Dudley Seymour, who bequeathed it to the Antiquarian and Landmarks Society in 1945. Restored and carefully maintained, the house looks much as it did when Barber visited in 1834.

CPB

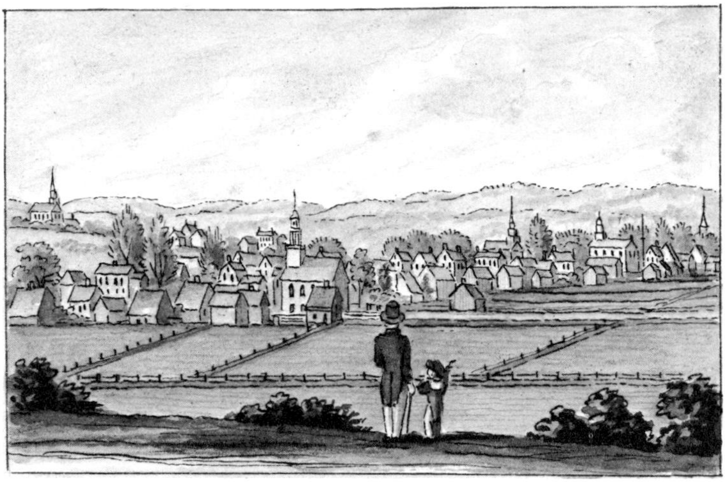

DANBURY

SOUTHEASTERN VIEW OF THE BOROUGH OF DANBURY

THIS VIEW WAS DRAWN, Barber tells us, from southeast of the town standing on the Norwalk Road. This was undoubtedly the Danbury-Norwalk Turnpike, incorporated in 1795, but by the 1830s abandoned by its proprietors to the public. It probably followed what is now Route 7 as far as about a mile north of Georgetown when it most likely took an easterly route along Simpaug Turnpike and on through Bethel to connect with South Street. The closest church to us is the Episcopal, built in 1763 and one of the few structures not burned by the British in 1777. Today South Street School occupies the site. The church on the extreme left is that of the Baptists. Barber was probably somewhere around Coalpit Hill to the south of Rogers Park.

CC

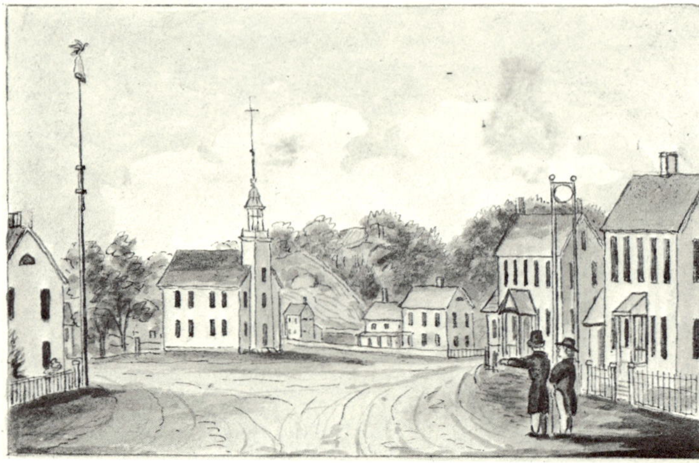

BETHEL
A VIEW OF THE
CONGREGATIONAL CHURCH IN BETHEL,
IN THE TOWN OF DANBURY

24

BETHEL WAS SET OFF in 1855, so was still part of Danbury when Barber drew this picture twenty years earlier. The Congregational church shown here was built in 1760 and burned in 1842. A larger one was constructed on the same site. In 1867 a third church was built, though moved a few yards and reoriented. The resolution directing the construction of the church in this drawing provided that it be forty-eight by thirty-six feet. The steeple must have been added sometime after 1820 or so, because P. T. Barnum (born 1810) recollected "The old meeting-house had neither steeple nor bell and was a plain edifice, comfortable enough in the summer, but my teeth chatter even now when I think of the dreary, cold, freezing hours passed in that place in winter." Using the graveyard to the left of the church and the hill behind it—both of which still exist—as landmarks, it appears that the new, much different church was rotated so as to face south instead of east as this one does. It is located at the crossing of Main, Prospect, and Maple streets.

CC

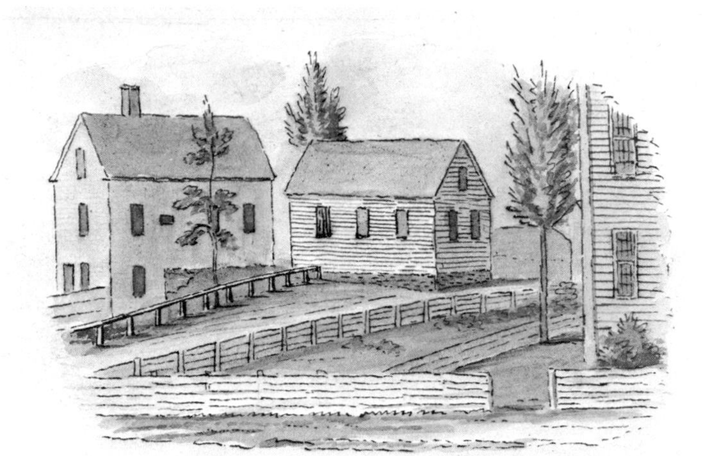

DANBURY

THE SANDEMANIAN CHURCH

ROBERT SANDEMAN (1718–1771) came from Scotland carrying principles that called for living a life exemplified by Jesus without reliance on professions of faith, thus differing from orthodox Congregationalists who proclaimed faith as the starting point of all godly lives. He established a small following in Boston and came to Danbury in 1764 and collected a second church there which he conducted at least until 1768. At the time this sketch was made, it was probably the only Sandemanian structure in the United States. Barber describes it as a "small, unostentatious building [which] very much resembles a common school house," clearly the structure in the center of this picture. Bailey in his *Danbury* said it was "glorified by its setting of green grass and tall trees upon the hilltop." It was still standing in the late 19th century, and Bailey includes a photograph of it. It was located near Terrace Place off a side street in the vicinity of the old Library on Main Street.

CC

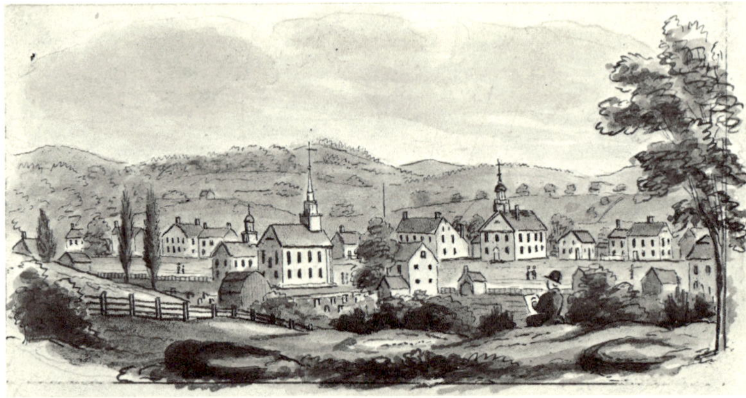

DANBURY

THE BOROUGH OF DANBURY

26 BOROUGH ORGANIZATION of the compact part of towns was instituted first at Bridgeport in 1801. Danbury's borough charter was granted in 1822, setting up a warden and six burgesses to administer the area, which in 1889 became the City of Danbury within the town. In 1965 the town and city were consolidated. This sketch, which Barber calls a "south view," was drawn from Deer Hill, perhaps a bit southwest of the present municipal building. The church in the foreground is that of the Universalists. To its right is the jail, behind which we can see the old burying ground where Robert Sandeman lies interred. It is still there, at the junction of Wooster and Main. To the left of the Universalist church is the Academy. Across the street is the county court house with a cupola. The old court house has been moved and stands south of the Wooster Street Cemetery to the rear of the Chevrolet dealership. It no longer wears its spire.

CC

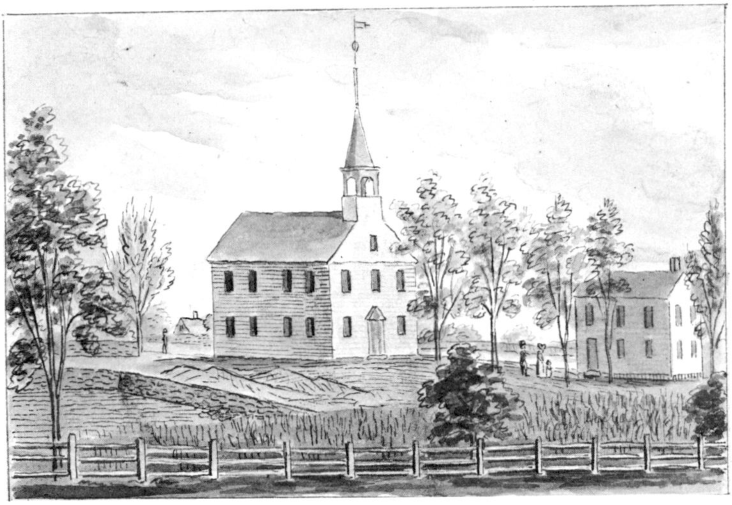

DARIEN

SOUTHWESTERN VIEW OF THE CONGREGATIONAL CHURCH

THE TOWN OF DARIEN was known as Middlesex Parish in Stamford until 1820 when it was established as a town and given a new name coined after the Isthmus of Darien. John Warner Barber visited the town on September 10, 1834 when he sketched what he later called "the ancient Congregational church." The structure that he drew was indeed ancient. The parish was established in 1737 and the church was completed seven years later in 1744. In 1781 pro-British Tories surrounded the meetinghouse and took all the men attending church, including the minister, Moses Mather, prisoners. It was five months, after much hardship and privation, before they were released. When Middlesex Parish became a town in 1820, the old wooden building became the town meetinghouse. Finally, in 1836 the old structure was torn down and a new brick meetinghouse, still standing, was erected on an adjacent lot.

CPB

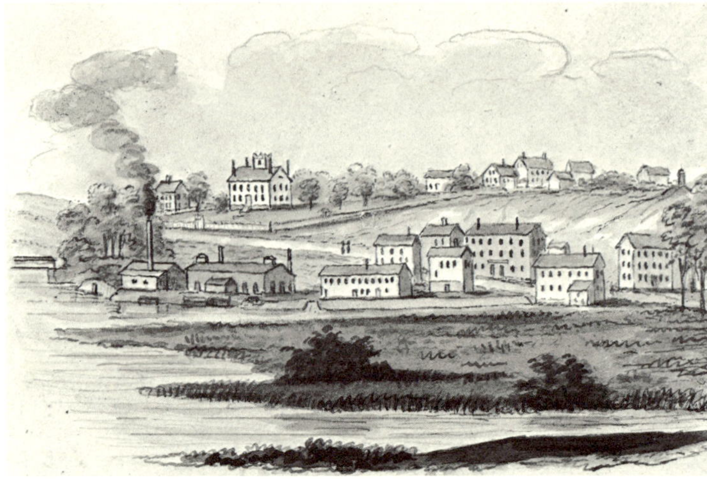

DERBY

SOUTHEAST VIEW OF DERBY LANDING

28 THIS VIEW OF DERBY LANDING, like so many of the scenes from Barber's time, has been completely altered. It must have been spectacular in the 1830s when you could look nearly straight down two hundred feet to the Housatonnic River below. The site, alongside Route 34 where you can still stand, was called the Landing because piers and docks had been built there to receive shipping bound for New York and the West Indies. Wooden pilings and stone abutments are still visible except at high tide.

Little else has survived. Oil tanks, the buildings of Petrol Plus and a Sunoco station have succeeded the Derby Lumber Company's yard and its predecessor, Hallock's boat yard. As late as 1935 at least a part of the house where Isaac Hull was born in 1775 was still standing, used as an office by the lumber company. The bridge in the background of Barber's view has given way to a more modern bridge, but a couple of railroad trestles and bridges connecting Routes 34 and 8 further obstruct the prospect. Possibly the only surviving structure from Barber's view may be a now uninhabited and derelict structure, not long for this world, at 10 Prospect Street, the road that in Barber's view is seen branching off to the east (right).

CC

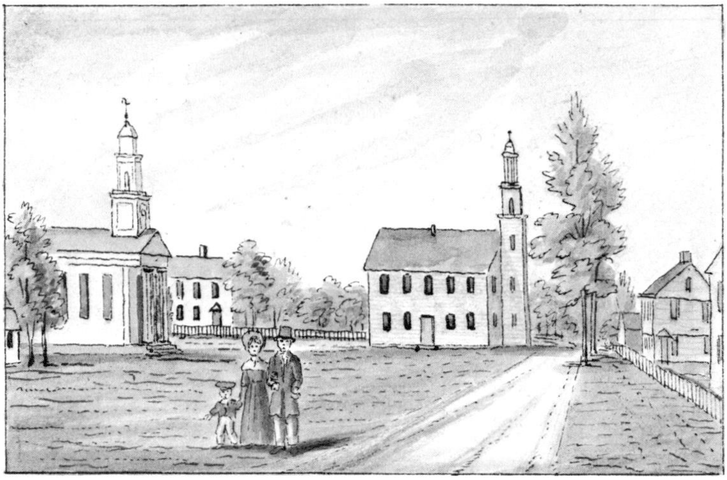

DURHAM

SOUTH VIEW OF THE

CHURCHES IN DURHAM

BARBER DID THIS ILLUSTRATION of the Green in 1835 when the town's third Congregational meetinghouse, shown at the left, had just been completed, and the earlier one, dating from 1736 and shown in the center, was about to be torn down. The new structure burned nine years later, and its replacement serves today at the Town Hall. The view is looking north on what is now Main Street (Route 17) at the Maple Avenue intersection. The house between the churches was built in 1803 for the Rev. David Smith, Yale 1795. He was the successor and son-in-law of the Rev. Elizur Goodrich, Yale 1752, whose home, erected in 1764, is at the right. Both residences survive today. Elizur Goodrich, Jr., Yale 1779, was professor of law at Yale and Mayor of New Haven from 1804 to 1822.

FMS, DFM

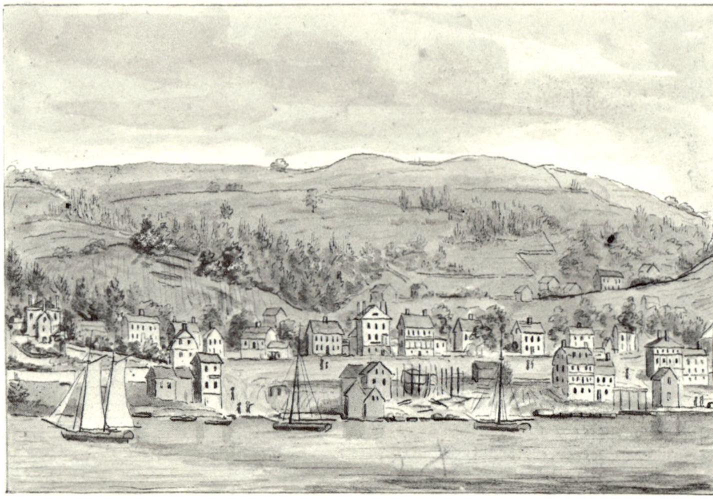

EAST HADDAM

WEST VIEW OF EAST HADDAM LANDING

30 East Haddam, probably best known today as the locale of Goodspeed Opera House, in Barber's day prospered mainly through cotton manufacturing and shipbuilding. A ship is shown under construction in the yard on the riverfront. Barber shows a stretch along what is now Route 149, some half mile north of the Opera House area. At the extreme left stands the General Epaphroditus Champion house with its near-by counting house. Champion, a General of the Connecticut Militia, had several vessels in the West Indies trade. Of the Champion House Barber says, "It is distinguished for its bold and lofty terraces, and is a striking object to travellers passing on the river." Built in 1794, it was patterned on the Deming House in Litchfield. For motorists driving north on Route 149 this house with its bold quoins and handsome Ionic porches, standing behind and above its counting house, is still an impressive sight. (Barber shows the four-windowed gable end of the counting house above some buildings near the river's edge.) Many of the homes shown here still stand, including almost all of them between the Champion House and the Timothy Green House with its half-moon gable-end in the center of the picture.

JBM

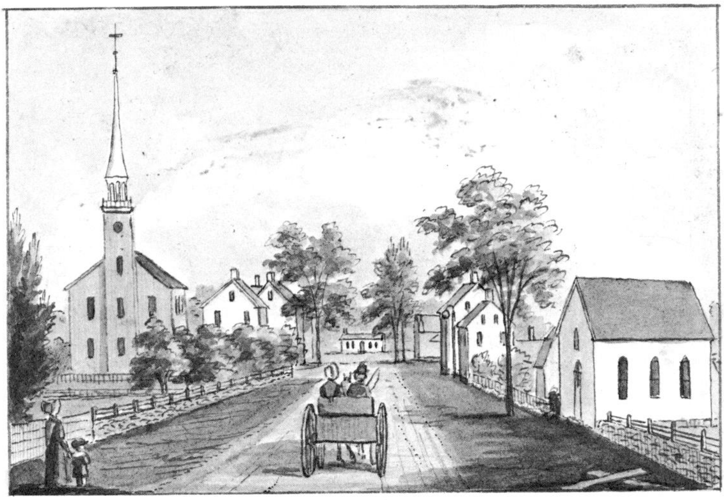

EAST HAVEN: NORTHWESTERN VIEW OF CONGREGATIONAL AND EPISCOPAL CHURCHES

THIS VIEW UP WHAT is now High Street shows the Congregational church, today called the Old Stone Meetinghouse, at the left facing Main Street. Opened for services in 1774 but not completed until 1796, it retains its original general appearance, but there have been some embellishments. The doors and windows have been somewhat altered, a belfry with a 196-foot spire was added in 1859, and a slate roof was put on in 1908. The Episcopal church, a small building with three windows at the far right, has disappeared, and a row of retail stores has replaced it. Beyond them and across High Street the Town Hall is located today. This site is a short distance from Route I-95 and can be approached from Exit 51 driving east and Exit 52 driving west toward New Haven.

FMS, DFM

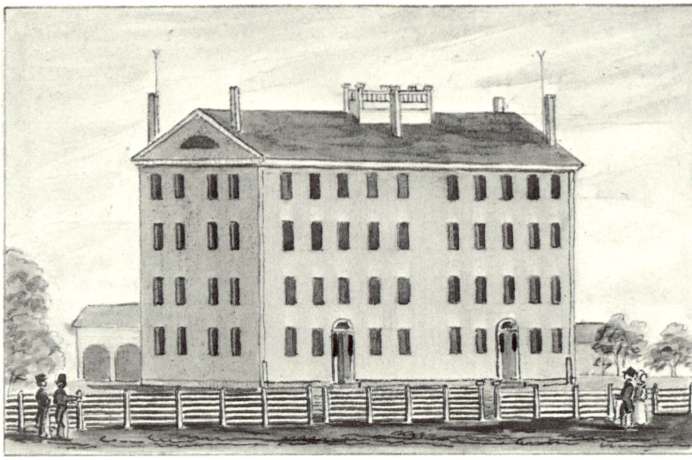

SOUTH WINDSOR
THEOLOGICAL INSTITUTE
AT EAST WINDSOR

32 THIS PORTION OF EAST WINDSOR is now South Windsor. The building was formerly on Main Street in the East Windsor Hill section. The building was demolished in 1936.

This seminary was founded by Congregational ministers who opposed certain doctrines taught at the Yale Divinity School. They felt that the sound doctrines of New England Calvinism, advanced by Edwards, Bellamy, and Dwight, were being discarded. The Theological Institute of Connecticut was founded in 1834 and the cornerstone of the building was the steppingstone from the local home of Timothy and Jonathan Edwards. Complaints by faculty and students of a lack of social and literary atmosphere in the town resulted in the seminary moving to Hartford in 1865 where it became the Hartford Theological Seminary.

Main Street is renowned for the fine Colonial, Federal and early Victorian houses, reflecting the wealth of the early tobacco growers.

CLR

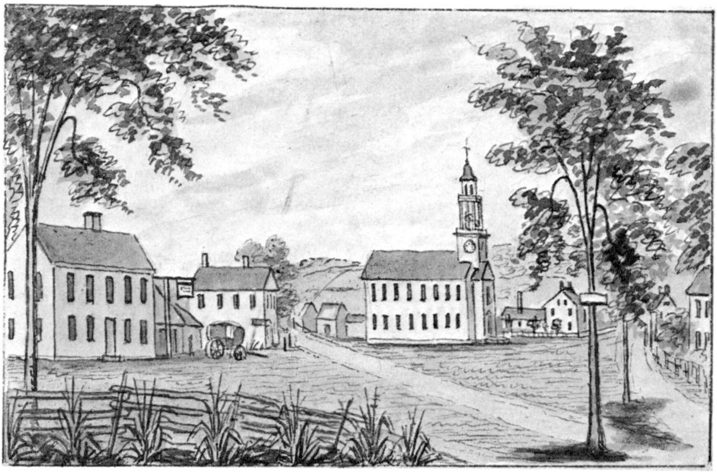

ELLINGTON

WESTERN VIEW OF THE CENTRAL PART

THE CONGREGATIONAL CHURCH shown in Barber's sketch is the second meeting house, erected in 1806 to replace the first, which was built in 1739. The second was moved to Rockville in 1868, where it was used as a public hall.

The third (and present) Congregational Church was erected in 1868 to replace the second.

The Ellington green can be reached by Route 286 from the south and Route 140 from the east and west. Barber's viewpoint was at the western end of the green, looking east.

DBE

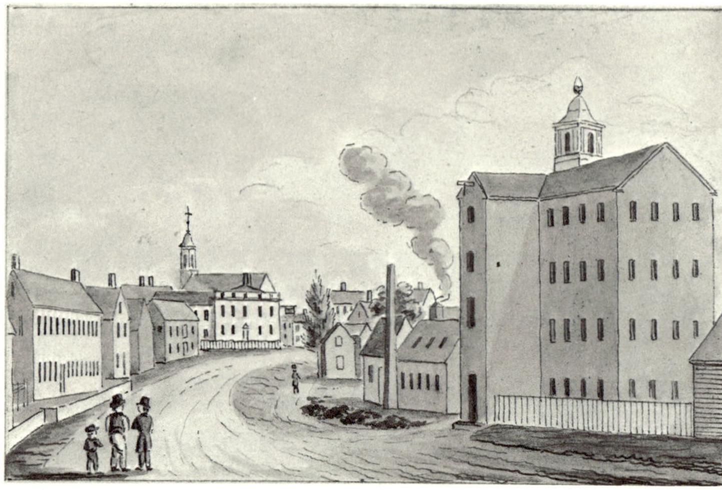

ENFIELD

THOMPSONVILLE

THE THOMPSONVILLE SECTION of the Town of Enfield borders the Connecticut River on the eastern side and is adjacent to Route 5. None of the structures shown by Barber remains.

Thompsonville was named after Orrin Thompson, 1788–1873, a native of Suffield who, after carpet store experience in New York, founded the first carpet factory along the local Freshwater River in 1828. The industry, due to a protective tariff, flourished over the next hundred years, the last major company being the Bigelow-Sanford Carpet Company. In recent years this company transferred production out-of-state and buildings were untenanted; now (1989) the buildings are in the process of being remodeled to condominium residences.

In 1642 a survey was ordered by the Massachusetts Bay General Court to establish a border between Massachusetts and Connecticut. In error the surveyors included the present town of Enfield in Massachusetts. After years of continuous controversy, caused by local residents who preferred the more liberal laws and lower taxes of Connecticut, the town was restored to Connecticut in 1749.

CLR

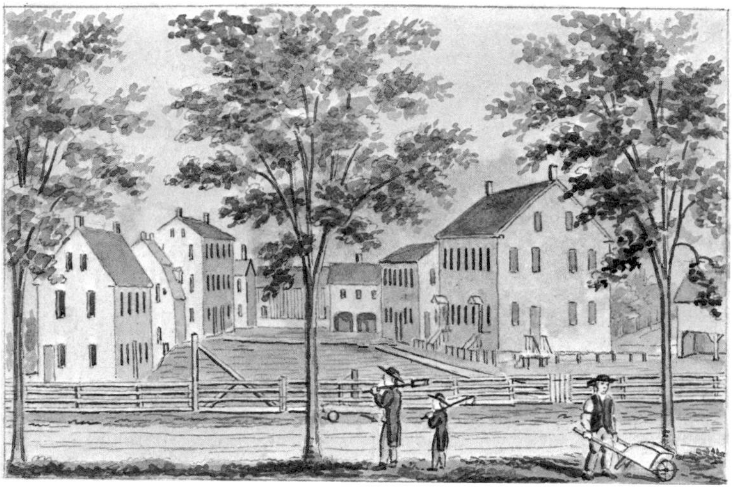

ENFIELD

SHAKER HOUSES

THE FORMER SHAKER COMMUNITY is found on Route 220, about five miles northeast of Enfield center. Only one house has been restored and is used by the State. The remains of the Community were purchased by the State of Connecticut in 1915 and became the Norris B. Osborn State Prison Farm.

About the year 1781, the Rev. Joseph Meacham, pastor of the Enfield Baptist Church, became one of the first American converts to Shakerism and with many of his former parishioners formed a Shaker Society at Enfield about 1788. This monastic society prospered and, as stated by Barber in 1836, the community totaled 200 persons divided into five families. The central part of the settlement is probably shown in Barber's view. In 1886 the society consisted of about 250 members divided into three families, and owned twenty-seven hundred acres, most under cultivation. They sustained their own schools, took no part in political affairs and were socially excluded from the town. Like most Shaker settlements, the community declined due to lack of new members and the older members moved to more active Shaker communities.

CLR

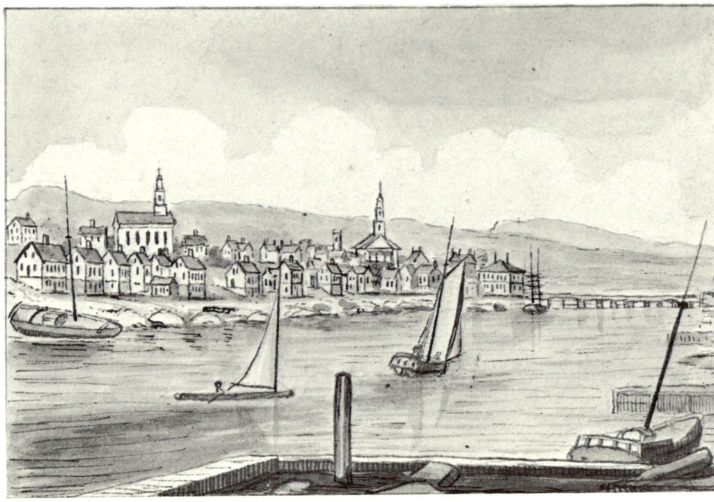

NEW HAVEN

SOUTH VIEW OF FAIR HAVEN

(WESTERN PART)

THE FAIR HAVEN SECTION of New Haven was in Barber's time a remote and rather self-contained neighborhood devoted largely to the then-thriving oystering industry. Shown here is a view looking toward the west from Quinnipiac Avenue across the Quinnipiac River near where it flows into New Haven Harbor. The East Pearl Street United Methodist Church is at the left, the First Congregational Church of Fair Haven on Grand Street (now Grand Avenue) is in the center, and the Grand Street (now Grand Avenue) bridge is at the far right. Both of the meetinghouses have been replaced since then, the Methodist in 1871 by a Victorian Gothic structure and the Congregational in 1853 by a red brick building. East Rock is seen in the distance at the right.

FMS, DFM

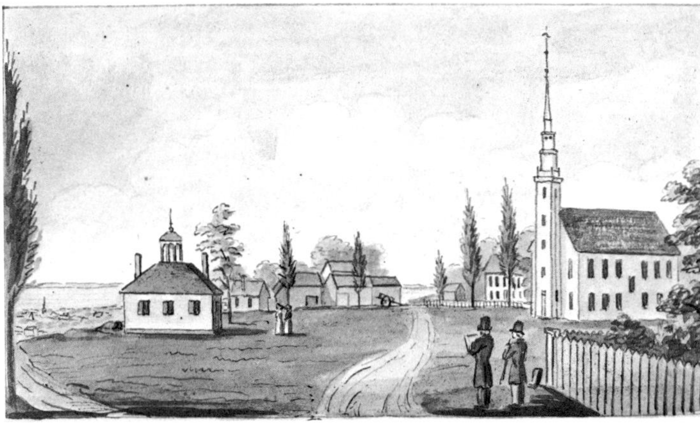

FAIRFIELD

NORTH VIEW OF THE ACADEMY AND CONGREGATIONAL CHURCH IN GREENFIELD HILL

THE STRUCTURES IN THIS PICTURE were built on the foundations of those they replaced after the British burned most of the town during their dastardly raid of July, 1779. The jail is on the left; the Congregational church on the right. In the center is the County Court House (1794), which also doubled as a town meeting hall. In 1853, after years of rancorous debate, the county court functions were transferred to Bridgeport, and the upstairs of the building was leased to the Fairfield Female Seminary; the rest became the Town House. The building was remodeled in Second Empire style in 1870, unremodeled in 1936, and subsequently given a very large addition. Barber would have been facing northwest with the Sun Tavern—built about 1783 and still standing—on his left. St. Paul's Church was built c. 1855 on the site of the old jail. Today the old Fairfield Academy (1804), next to the Burr Mansion on the Old Post Road, sits just south of St. Paul's, moved there in the early 1950s. The north side of the Town House looks much as Barber shows the south side here; but the side he shows has been completely blocked by a great wing built in 1957. It remains in use today. A plaque by the front door delightfully tells us of a visit by President Ronald Reagan in 1984.

CC

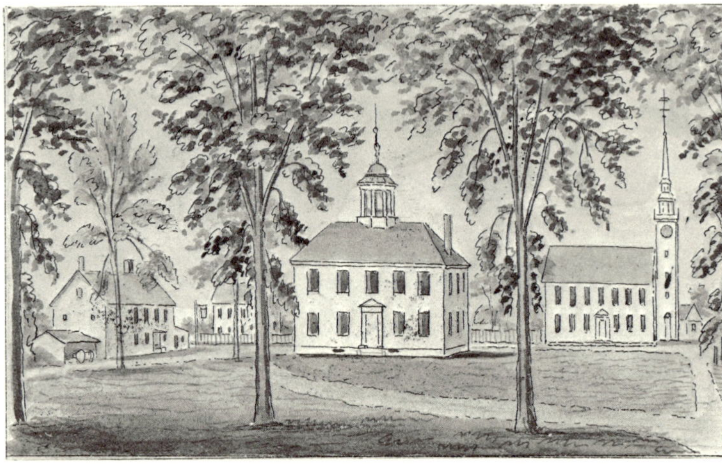

FAIRFIELD: EASTERN VIEW OF THE COURT HOUSE, CONGREGATIONAL CHURCH, AND JAIL IN FAIRFIELD

38 THIS VIEW OF GREENFIELD HILL in Fairfield shows the church and academy made famous by Timothy Dwight. Later president of Yale, Dwight wrote a long poem, "Greenfield Hill," describing life here at the end of the 18th century as Dwight would have liked it to be (and perhaps thought it was), and which established the stereotype of the pre-industrial New England village. Barber calls attention to the spire of the Fairfield Congregational church, and a squint through a magnifying glass reveals the whole church. There were many fewer trees in Connecticut in the 19th century than there are today, and thus more long views. Indeed, Samuel Goodrich said that in 1810 or so he could see that same spire from his father's house on a hill just southwest of the center of Ridgefield! The site of the Academy is marked by a plaque—nearly obscured by Bar Harbor Junipers—in the island formed by Bronson, Old Academy, and Hillside roads. The church pictured here was built in 1762; the Academy in 1786. The present church, built in 1854, was entirely remodeled in the 1940s so as to bear little resemblance to its original appearance.

CC

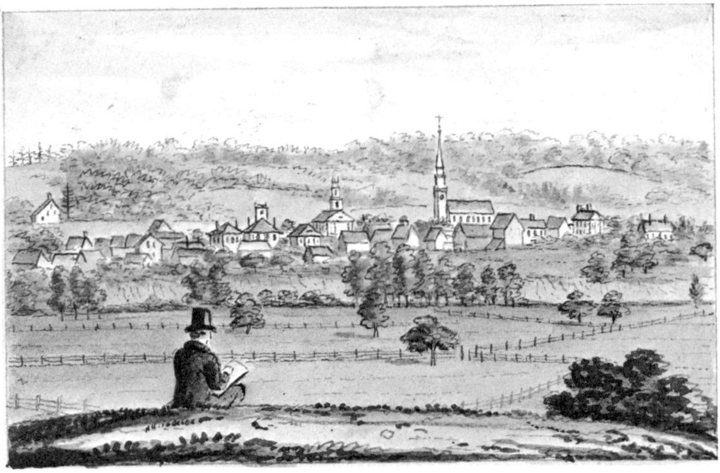

FARMINGTON
NORTHWEST VIEW
FROM ROUND HILL

JOHN WARNER BARBER selected as his vantage point a site located to the west of the center of Farmington known as Round Hill, a mound of earth and sand in the middle of a meadow. The river itself is obscured by a line of trees as is the Farmington Canal opened in 1828. Running parallel to the river and canal are two streets, the most important of which, is Main Street. The tallest spire belongs to the First Congregational Church built by Judah Woodruff in 1771. Next to it, to the north, is a Methodist church completed the previous year. Further to the north are the town hall and Union Hotel constructed around 1830 to serve the canal trade which briefly made Farmington an inland port. Much of the old center of Farmington has been preserved, but the elevated site where Barber took his sketch was gradually eroded as a result of the need for sand and gravel. The Congregational Church, widely recognized as one of the most handsome in New England, is well preserved. The Union Hotel was acquired by Miss Sarah Porter for her famous school and still stands, but the Methodist church was burned in 1897.

CPB

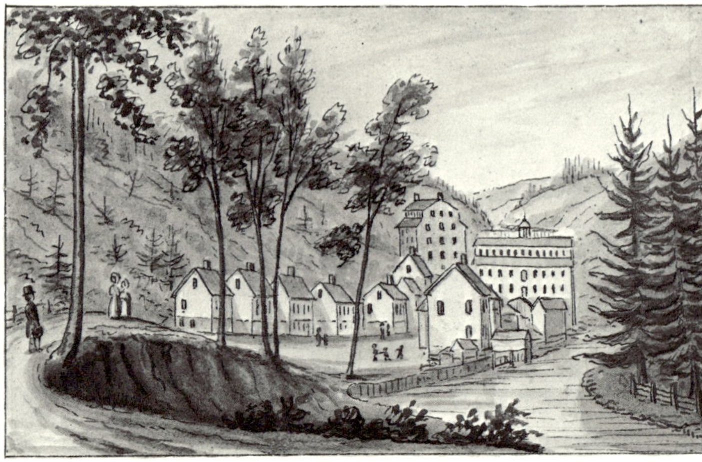

GLASTONBURY

COTTON FACTORY VILLAGE

40 ROARING BROOK FLOWS past mills and workers' houses in Cotton Hollow, South Glastonbury. The two largest buildings are Pardon Brown's woollen mill (c. 1804) and, to its left, the cotton mill (c. 1814) of the Hartford Manufacturing Company, the ruins of which still stand. Behind the cupola of Brown's mill appears the rim of a fifty-foot dam, water from which (and from a smaller dam below it) powered both mills. The two dams together provided the highest falls for manufacturing purposes in New England. Weakened by floods, the high dam was dynamited, for safety, in 1904. The artist was looking east from a position on Roaring Brook a quarter of a mile east of Route 17. Barber's view is now masked by trees, but some of the buildings can still be seen in a pleasant walk along Cotton Hollow Road.

JBM

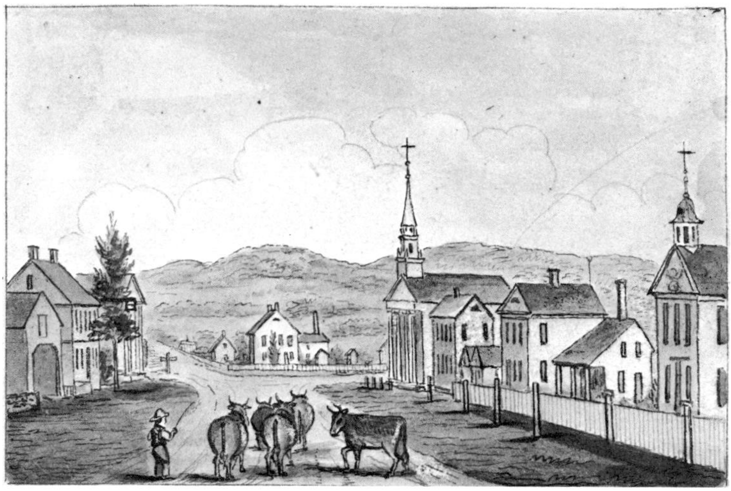

GOSHEN

SOUTH VIEW OF CENTRAL PART

THE COWS IN THIS SCENE amble along what is now Connecticut Route 63 toward its junction with Route 4. The church, here shown with a tall spire, today has a shorter domed cupola. There is a parking lot beside the church. The house on the right with its gable end facing the street is still there, though the buildings on either side of it have gone, one of these, the one shown next to the church, having been a brick structure that served as the common district schoolhouse. At the far right, the building with the cupola presently houses the Goshen Historical Society. It was in Barber's time known as the Academy where, as he reports, "the higher branches of education are taught." The house at the left still stands, though with the addition of two large dormers facing the street.

JBM

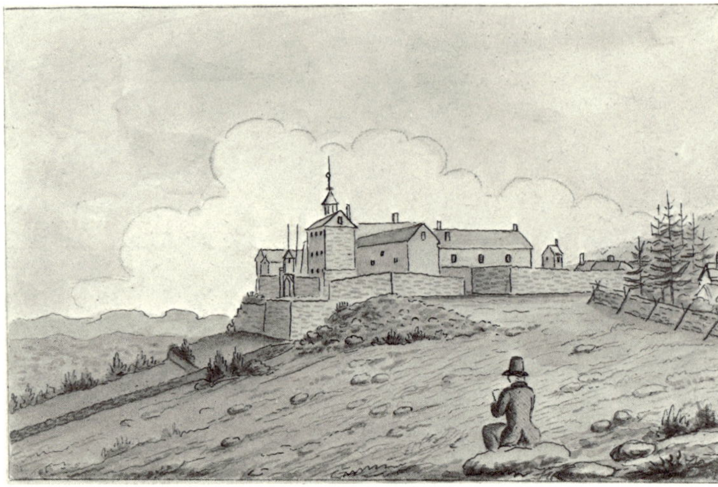

GRANBY

SOUTH VIEW OF NEWGATE PRISON BUILDINGS

SINCE THE 1960s Newgate Prison, the site of the first chartered copper mine in America in 1707, has been a state museum and a National Historic Landmark. During the Revolution it served as a prison for captured British soldiers and until 1827 as Connecticut's first state prison.

Visitors can see the two main shafts where prisoners were quartered, the four-story brick and stone cell block, the guardhouse, and the blacksmith and cooper shops. Also the dreaded treadmill which inmates had to operate in 11-minute shifts. Most imposing is the wall around the yard, 16 feet high and four and one-half feet thick.

The town road now passes on the east side, the craggy rocks are as lofty as ever, but the valleys on the west are covered with trees. The prison lies a couple of miles north of Route 20 between East Granby and Granby. East Granby became a separate town in 1858. The museum is open from mid-May to October 31st, Wednesday to Sunday.

ESG

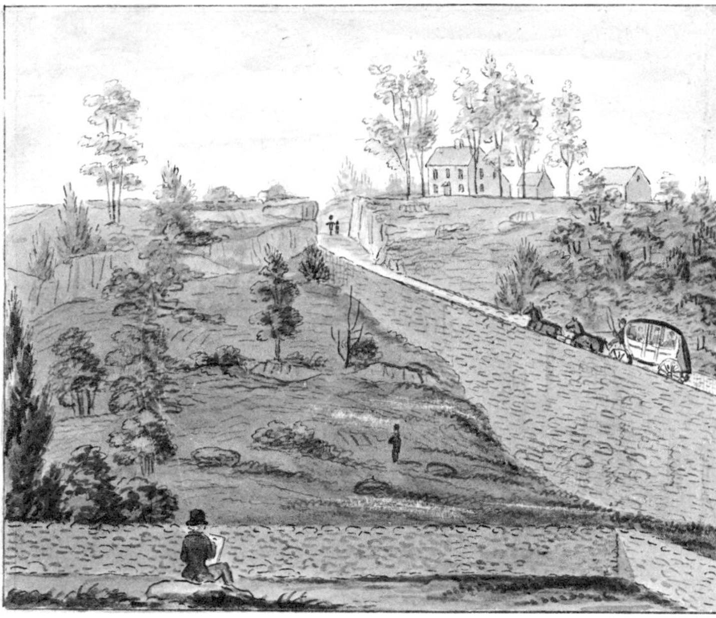

GREENWICH

SOUTHEASTERN VIEW OF PUTNAM'S HILL

GREENWICH WAS KNOWN as Horse Neck until just about the turn of the 19th century, and Barber refers to this scene, at Put's Hill, as in West Greenwich. This view shows the site of the famous flight of General Israel Putnam from a British attack in February, 1779. Tradition has Putnam spurring his horse down a flight of 74 stone steps set in the steep hill where the trees show here. There was also a cow path there, and it is more likely that he followed that. The cut through the rocks was made some time in the early 19th century, and the road—the old Post Road—relocated at the same time. The causeway shown here still exists as part of the Post Road. Barber was standing somewhere around 17 Mallard Drive which runs parallel to the Post Road off Overlook Drive at the bottom of the declivity. A stone monument marks the place where Putnam is supposed to have begun his gallop down the steps. A few steps of a set blasted in the rock in 1902 are still usable. A couple of hundred yards to the west is the Knapp Tavern where tradition has Putnam shaving when, in his mirror, he saw the Lobsterbacks approaching. The Tavern, built in 1690, is maintained as a museum by the Putnam Hill chapter of the D.A.R.

CC

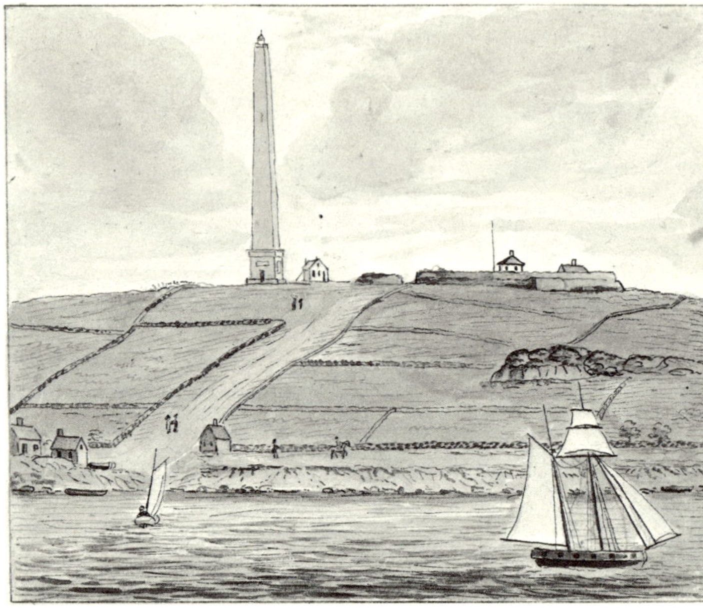

GROTON: GROTON MONUMENT AND FORT GRISWOLD

STILL THE DOMINANT skyline feature of the east bank of the Thames River in Groton, the granite Monument was erected in 1830 to commemorate the bloody Battle of Fort Griswold on September 6, 1781. Under Benedict Arnold, the British first burned New London, then crossed the river, overwhelming the fort and massacring its defenders. The view is from the vicinity of Amtrak's Shaw's Cove bridge, reached from Bank Street just south of New London's waterfront business district. Today the Monument looks down on the historic section of the City of Groton known as Groton Bank, and may be reached from the Bridge Street exit of Interstate 95 eastbound, or the Submarine Base exit westbound. A splendid view of New London, the Thames, and Long Island Sound rewards those who seek out this historic and hallowed place.

BR

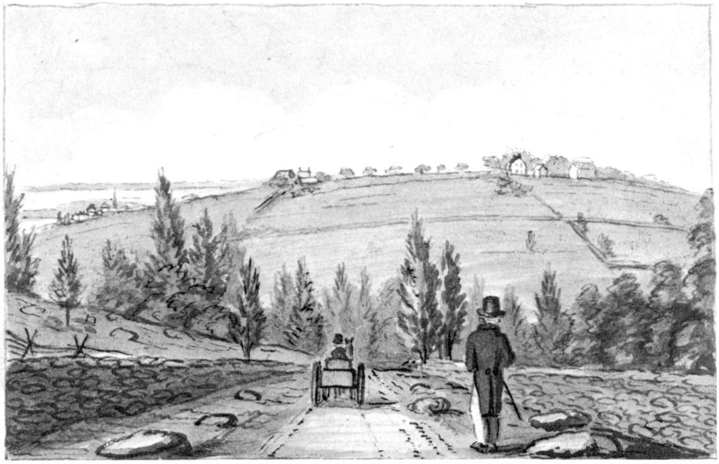

GROTON

NORTH VIEW OF PEQUOT HILL

FROM COW HILL, the artist is looking south at the high ground formerly known as Pequot Hill because of the Indian fort that once commanded it. In 1637 this was the site of the first conflict between the English, under Capt. John Mason, and the Pequots. Virtually all of this land came to be owned by the Fish family. The Roswell Fish house, right, burned just before World War II after being struck by lightning. The 1798 Alden Fish house, left, is still occupied by Fish descendants and the family cemetery may be seen nearby on Pequot Avenue, off Sandy Hollow Road at the Allyn Street interchange of Interstate 95. The 1829 Mariner's Free Church spire rises above the buildings of Mystic at the left on a site now occupied by the Union Baptist Church. Mason's Island lies beyond the village, with Fisher's Island in the distance.

BR

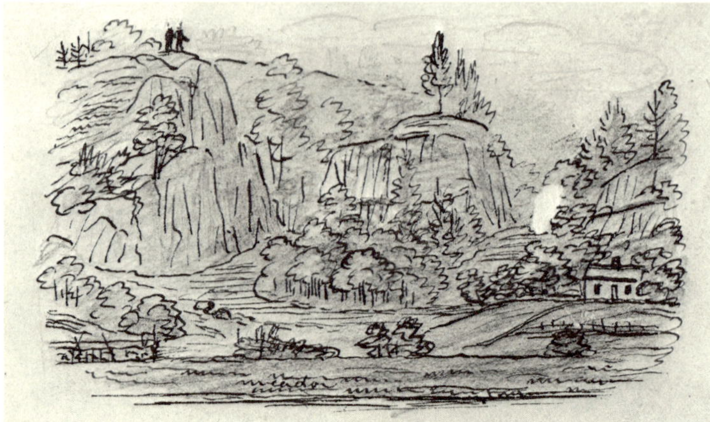

GROTON

SOUTH VIEW OF PORTER'S ROCKS

46 NOW LARGELY HIDDEN by trees, these rocky cliffs on the west side of the Mystic River are two miles north of the center of Mystic on River Road, reached via Pearl Street, and less than a mile south of Route 27 in Old Mystic. From outcroppings on the private land at the top they afford an expansive view of the Mystic River area. Granite quarried here in the early 19th century was shipped by schooner to coastal sites for breakwaters and piers. The origin of the name is unknown, there having been no Porter family in the area. The Zipporah Wells house no longer stands.

BR

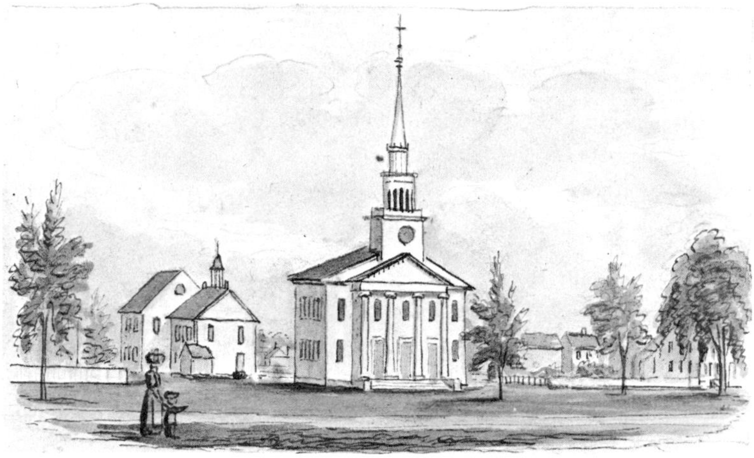

GUILFORD
CONGREGATIONAL CHURCH

THE FIRST CONGREGATIONAL CHURCH, seen from the middle of the Guilford Green facing away from the shore, dominates this scene as it did in Barber's illustration. It was built in 1830, the third meetinghouse to serve the congregation. The William Redfield house, dating from 1751 and completely obscured by the tree and fence at the far left, is still there, but the building called the Town House and the Academy, both seen beyond the pedestrians, have been replaced by a store. A handsome residential structure was built to the right of the church late in the last century, and the house at the far right has since been moved to another lot. The Green is only three country blocks toward the Sound from Exit 58 on Route I-95 and one block beyond the Boston Post Road (Route 1).

FMS, DFM

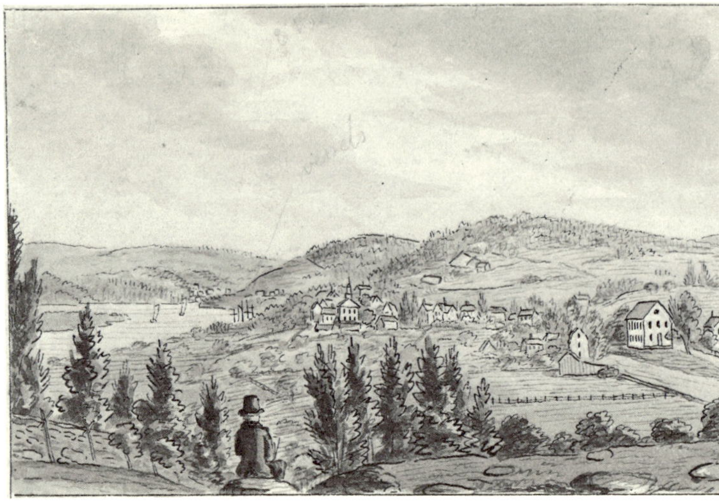

HADDAM

NORTHWEST VIEW

48 A MILE BELOW HIGGANUM CENTER, southbound travelers on the Middlesex Turnpike found themselves climbing away from the Connecticut River toward the high ground of Barber's view. The picturesque scene of river and hills, taken from a yet higher vantage point several hundred feet east of what is now Walkley Hill Road, is almost completely obscured in summer by mature trees; glimpses of the hills beyond East Haddam and the dome of the Connecticut Yankee Atomic Power Plant are the only reminders of the river and its valley below. Walkley Hill Road drops down to Haddam Center within a half-mile of this point, rejoining Saybrook Road (Route 154) at the site of the 1829 court house. This building, later the town hall, burned down in 1929. A historical marker and flagpole stand adjacent to the granite tablet marking the court house location. The Haddam Historical Society's Thankful Arnold House (ca. 1794–1810) stands nearby.

BR

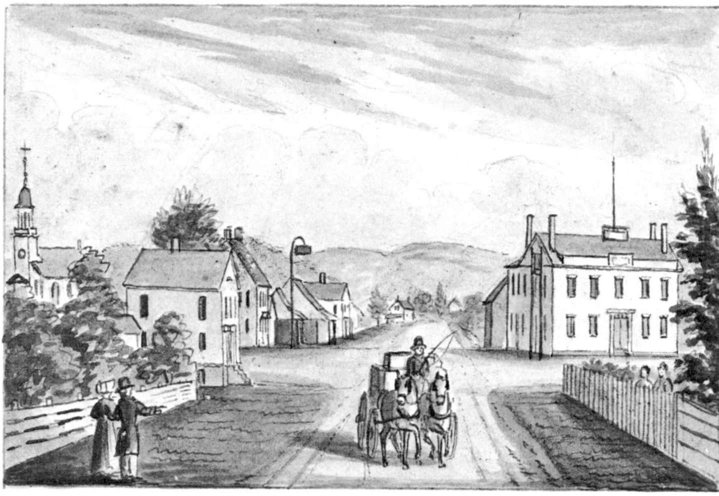

HAMDEN

CENTRAL PART

THE HORSES IN THIS illustration are headed toward New Haven down what is today Whitney Avenue, and they have just passed the Dixwell Avenue intersection. Grace Episcopal Church, erected in the Federal style in 1821 and attributed to the builder David Hoadley, is seen at the left. A new steeple was added in 1921, and in 1966 the building was moved to a new location across Dixwell Avenue, so that it now faces north rather than south as it did originally. All the other structures depicted by Barber are gone. A large and handsome red brick town Hall stands on the northwest corner of the intersection, and offices and stores fill the rest of the space. This site can be reached by coming off the Wilbur Cross Parkway (Route 15) at Exit 62.

FMS, DFM

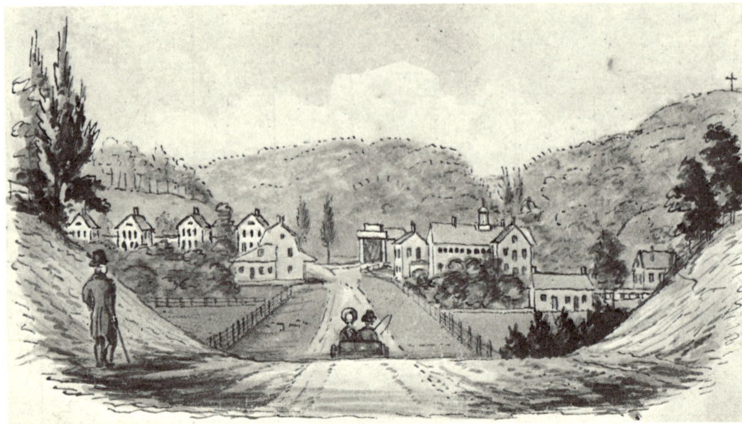

HAMDEN

SOUTH VIEW OF WHITNEYVILLE

50 Eli Whitney, already famous as the inventor of the cotton gin, purchased land along the Mill River in 1798. There he established the Whitney Armory, which manufactured firearms, and the village that grew around it became known as Whitneyville. This view toward the north up what is now Whitney Avenue just north of the New Haven line shows the factory buildings on the east side of the road and the northern face of East Rock further to the right. Mr. Whitney's barn, built in 1816, is across the road, and beyond it are houses for his employees. Only the barn and a boardinghouse for single workers survive today. The truss bridge in the center, leading to what is now Davis Street, was erected in 1824 using a design patented by the distinguished New Haven architect, Ithiel Town.

FMS, DFM

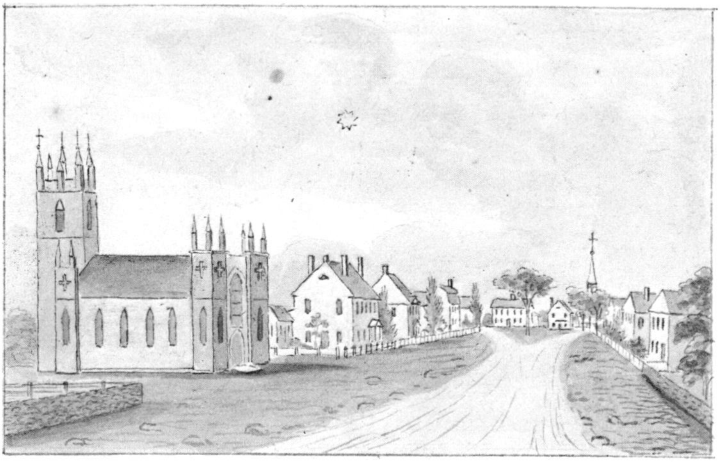

HEBRON
SOUTH VIEW
(CENTRAL PART)

BARBER'S SKETCH OF HEBRON bears a remarkable resemblance to the view today, despite the passage of time and the great fire of 1882.

St. Peter's Episcopal Church (1826), at the left of the drawing still stands, minus the spires, and is still in use. The dwelling (1806) of John S. Peters, a former Governor, looks much the same and is still a private residence.

The next house is the Amos Bassett house (1794), recently restored. The next two buildings no longer stand. A synagogue is now next the Bassett house. The house at the end was a store and post office in Barber's time. In its place is a small park with war memorials.

Behind the tree at the fork in the road were the Handee house and store that burned in the fire of 1882. They were replaced by the Lord house, which became a store eventually and was torn down when Route 85 was built. A traffic light now operates about where the elm tree stood.

The Congregational Church shown to the right of the Handee house and store was also destroyed in the 1882 fire, was rebuilt on the same spot, and is still in use.

Barber's viewpoint was looking north on Church Street (Route 85) toward where Route 66 crosses.

DBE

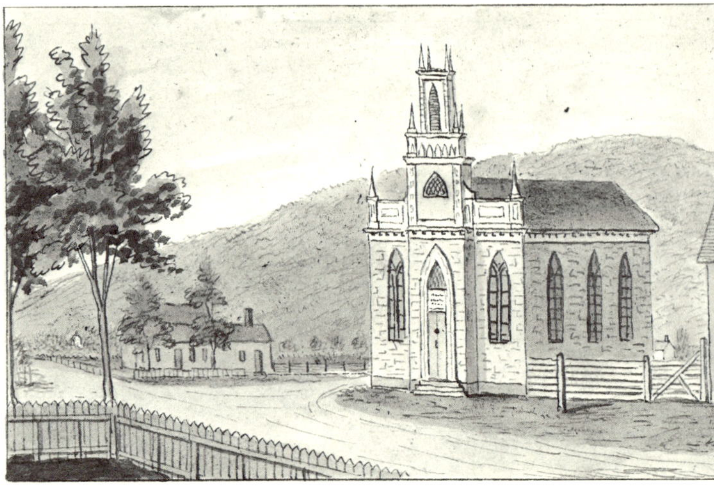

KENT

NORTHEASTERN VIEW OF

THE EPISCOPAL CHURCH

St. Andrew's in Kent stands at the intersection of state Routes 341 and 7, at one end of a shopping area that features a number of boutiques. A carved plaque above the door of the stone-and-brick church reads "St. Andrew's Church, A.D. 1826." In Connecticut, early-19th-century Episcopal churches were often, like this one, of Gothic Revival style.

The walls of St. Andrew's remain much as Barber pictured them, but the parts above the eave-line have been much altered. Barber shows a well-proportioned two-tiered square tower, the lower tier having a roughly triangular window. The four corners of both towers feature small pinnacles. The tower is flanked by wooden screens, each of these, again, capped by a pinnacle.

Today, the flanking screens are gone and the square tower, sheathed in wide clapboards, is shorter and squatter, rising in a series of four low tiers, each flared at the base. The window is no longer triangular but tall and narrow, with diamonded lights. On the ground, the rail fence shown by Barber is gone. The effect of all these changes is substantially to alter the appearance of the whole building.

JBM

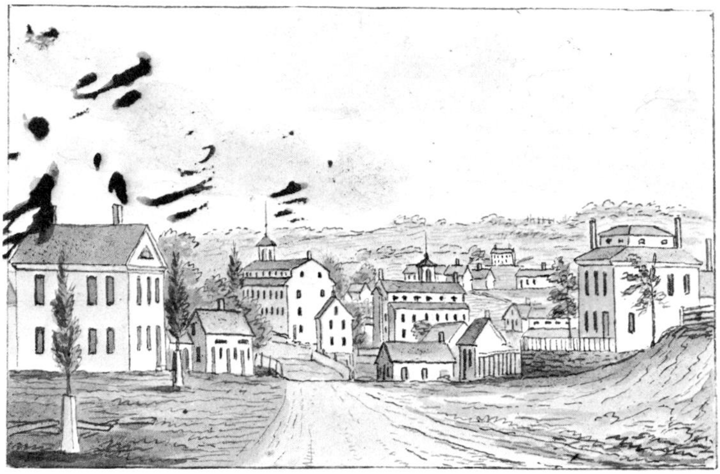

KILLINGLY

WESTERN VIEW OF DANIELSONVILLE

OF THE VARIOUS settlements in Killingly called by Barber "the greatest cotton manufacturing town in the State," the artist chose to draw Danielsonville, once known as West Killingly. He stood to the west of the Five Mile River, on the Brooklyn road, looking across the bridge to the village and to the Danielsonville cotton factory in the center. The picture he presents is of a prosperous, busy community. Today, a much widened Route 6 enters Danielson from the west and links with Route 12 which runs north and south. Some mill housing has survived, but there is little evidence in the center of town of structures dating from the earliest industrialization of the area. A later factory, now occupied by small commercial firms, stands at the approach to Danielson from the west. A depressed community in an economically stagnant part of the state, Danielson is now benefiting from the growth of northeastern Connecticut.

CPB

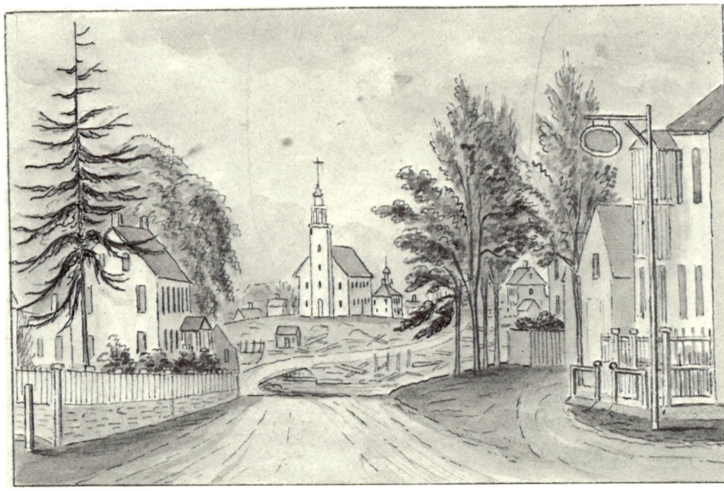

CLINTON

WEST VIEW OF KILLINGWORTH

(CENTRAL PART)

54 THIS VIEW OF MEETINGHOUSE HILL, looking eastward along what is now the Boston Post Road (Route 1) near where it crosses the Indian River, shows the First Church of Christ (Congregational) and the Academy immediately to its right. The meetinghouse was built in 1837, enlarged and remodeled in 1857 and 1877, and redecorated extensively in 1946. The Academy, now called the Grange Hall, was erected in 1801. Originally a school, it eventually became town property and is now used for various public meetings. The best-known colonial resident of Killingworth, whose home is seen at the right between the trees across the street from these buildings, was the Reverend Jared Eliot, a physician and brilliant scientist as well as a clergyman. The southern part of Killingworth, including this area, became the separate town of Clinton in 1838.

FMS, DFM

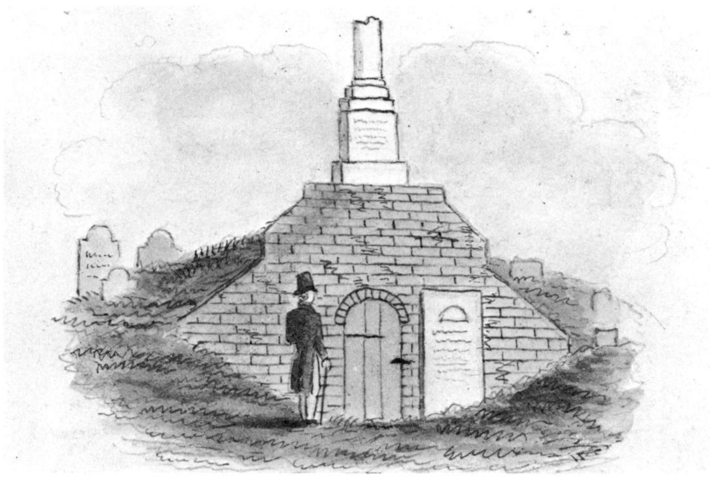

LEBANON

TOMB OF THE TRUMBULL FAMILY

THE CENTRAL FEATURE of Barber's sketch, the Congregational meeting house designed in 1804 by John Trumbull, the son of Governor Jonathan Trumbull, still dominates the green. Victorianized in 1871 and nearly destroyed when the 1938 hurricane toppled the steeple into the interior, it was fully restored to its original beauty by 1954, thanks to a state-wide campaign instituted by Governor Wilbur Cross.

At the left edge of the sketch, and still standing, is Redwood, the house built for middle Trumbull son David, by local artisan Isaac Fitch in 1778. Barber seems to have mis-identified this house as the William Williams house, which still stands at the southeast corner of the green, out of Barber's drawing. The next house is not identifiable. Beyond this is Governor Trumbull's office building, which became the famous War Office during the Revolution. In the distance beyond the War Office is Governor Trumbull's house erected in about 1755 and still standing.

Barber's viewpoint is at the south end of a green that extends for close to a mile. The viewpoint can be reached by Route 87 from Columbia and Norwich, Route 289 from Willimantic, Route 207 from Franklin, and Routes 16 and 207 from Colchester.

DBE

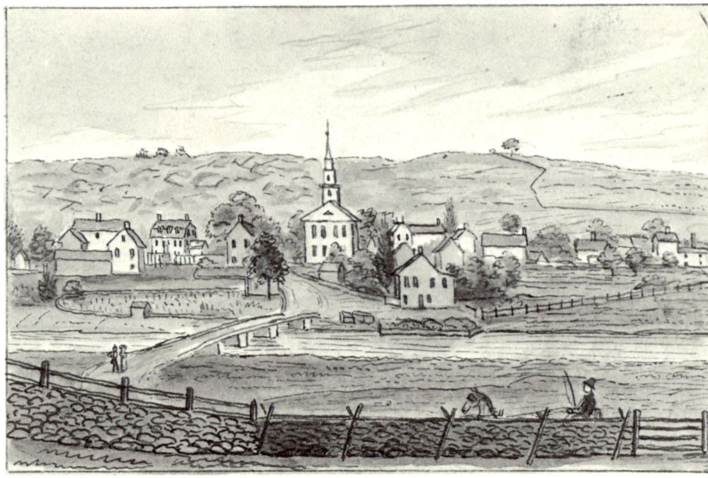

LYME

WEST VIEW

56 THE CONGREGATIONAL CHURCH the visitor to Old Lyme sees today is not the one shown by Barber, but a faithful replica of it, completed in 1910. The original 1817 church burned to the ground in 1907. The church stands where the original did, on Lyme Street at Ferry Road, which is the road leading to the bridge over the Lieutenant River in Barber's view. In 1855 this section of Lyme was incorporated as South Lyme, and in 1857 it took the name Old Lyme. Barber did this scene from near the point where Route 156 now crosses Lieutenant River. Today, trees and new development mask a good deal of what he shows of the church and the buildings near it, though most of them are still there. On his pencil sketch Barber notes "smooth" in the area on the far side of the stream to the right of the bridge, and "cornfield" in the area left of the bridge, the latter a reminder to himself to include the stubble that appears in his ink wash.

JBM

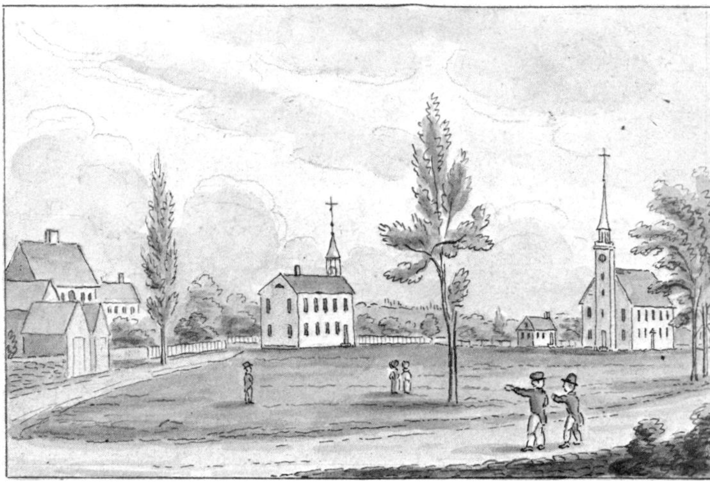

MADISON

LEE'S ACADEMY AND CONGREGATIONAL CHURCH

SHOWN IN THIS ILLUSTRATION are Lee Academy, built in 1821, in the center and the Congregational church at the right. This view, looking eastward just off the Boston Post Road in the central part of Madison, is much altered today. Lee Academy has survived and is now owned by the Madison Historical Society, but the Town Hall stands on the land once occupied by the meetinghouse. The present First Congregational church, dedicated in 1838, is at the left where the unidentified buildings stood, and a parish house is located between it and the Academy. To get to this site leave Route I-95 at Exit 61 and drive three country blocks toward Long Island Sound on Route 79 to the Boston Post Road (Route 1).

FMS, DFM

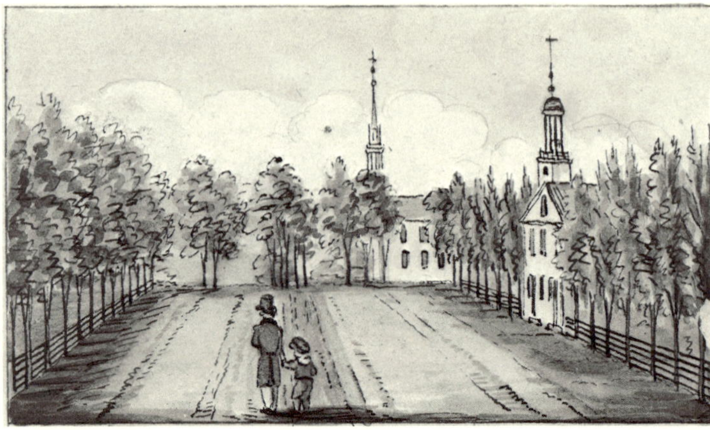

MANCHESTER
METHODIST AND
CONGREGATIONAL CHURCHES

58 THE CONGREGATIONAL CHURCH shown in the Barber drawing was sold to the town in 1879 for $700 to be used as a town hall. The structure was moved slightly to the west. The first floor was altered for offices, while the second floor became a hall for town meetings. The building no longer exists. In the same year a new church was built on the site of the old church. Twenty-five years later (1904) the current building was erected on the same site and still stands at what is now 11 Center Street.

The Methodist church in Barber's sketch is no longer there. As Manchester grew, a friendly division of the church occurred in 1851, with the original church moving south and a new church being created in the north end of town, reflecting the growth of industry at both ends of town. Presently at the site of what was the first Methodist church is the post office, an automobile dealer and retail shops.

Barber's viewpoint is looking west toward the present intersection of Center and Main streets. It can be reached by Routes 6 and 44 (running together) from the east and west and Route 83 from the north and south.

DBE

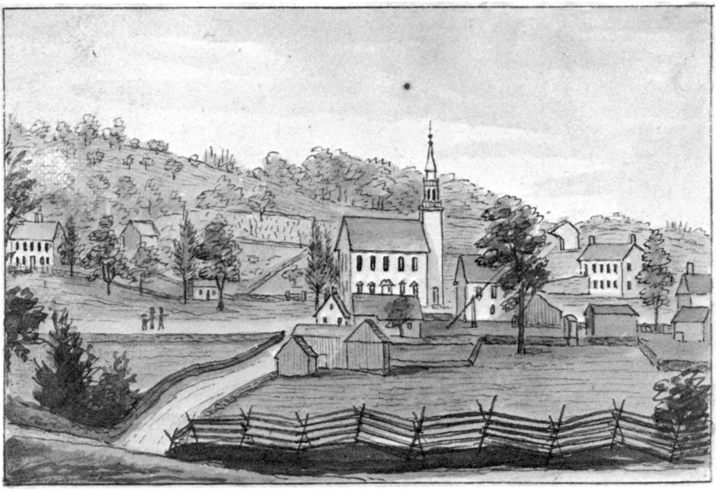

MANSFIELD

NORTHEAST VIEW OF THE PRESBYTERIAN CHURCH

BARBER'S DESIGNATION of the church in his sketch as Presbyterian was only partially correct: the first Congregational church in Mansfield was organized in 1710. Barber's woodcut shows the second Congregational church building erected in 1754. This building burned in 1866 and the present church building, designed by local architect/builder, Edwin S. Fitch, was erected in the same year on the same site. The 1866 church is still standing on what is now Mansfield Center, at 549 Storrs Road (Route 195). Barber's viewpoint is on Storrs Road looking north toward the center. The other buildings in his sketch are not identifiable.

A great controversy occurred between 1797 and 1805 during the pastorate of the Reverend John Sherman. Arriving as a Congregationalist, he soon revealed himself as a Unitarian. In order for the congregation to escape being brought to trial he persuaded the majority of his flock to adopt a Presbyterian form of government. Elders ruled the church in place of deacons until 1833, about the time that Barber identified the church as Presbyterian. After 1833 the church became fully Congregationalist again.

DBE

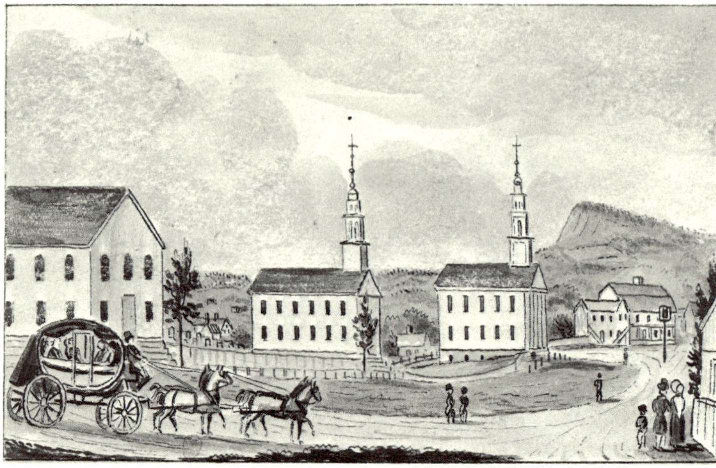

MERIDEN
SOUTHERN VIEW OF THE CHURCHES

IN THIS ILLUSTRATION three churches and a tavern line what is now Broad Street (Route 5), and Mount Lamentation can be seen three miles to the north beyond the town. The Episcopal church at the left is no longer there, and a funeral parlor has replaced it. Next toward the right is the First Baptist church. The present meetinghouse was erected in 1848. The third building from the left is Center Congregational Church, built in 1831, which is still standing. The tavern, immediately beyond what is now Main Street and which no longer exists, was for years a favorite resting spot for travelers, because it was exactly half way between New Haven and Hartford. Today a green strip up the middle of Broad Street is decorated with several handsome memorials to the veterans of various wars.

FMS, DFM

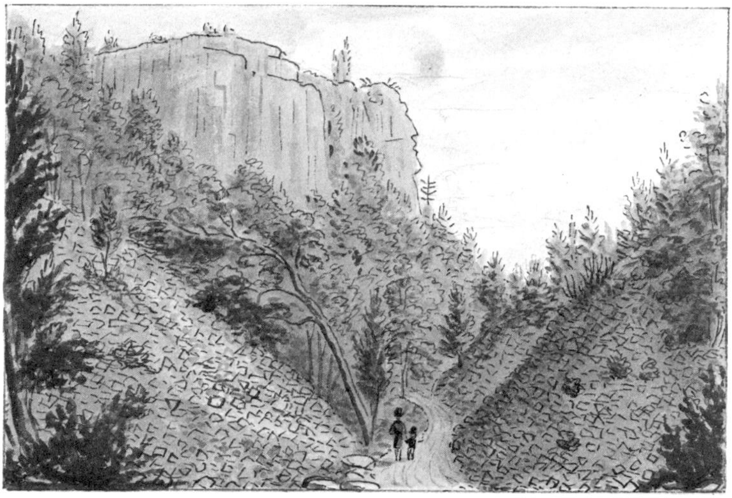

MERIDEN

NORTH VIEW OF THE CAT HOLE PASS

BARBER MADE THIS rendering facing north from what is now Kensington Avenue near its terminus at Chamberlain Highway in a mountainous area in northwestern Meriden. The Cat Hole Pass is between South Mountain and Cat Hole Mountain, and the illustration focused on a picturesque feature which has disappeared due to erosion in the intervening century and a half. There was then a perpendicular rock which, the text explained, had "the appearance of a profile of the human face" and which was "thought by some to resemble in a slight degree the profile of Washington, the Father of his country." The site can be reached by driving east on Route 66 from Routes 84 or 10 or west on Route 66 from Routes 5, 15 or I-91. Turn north onto Chamberlain Highway (Route 71) and then go right onto Kensington Avenue.

FMS, DFM

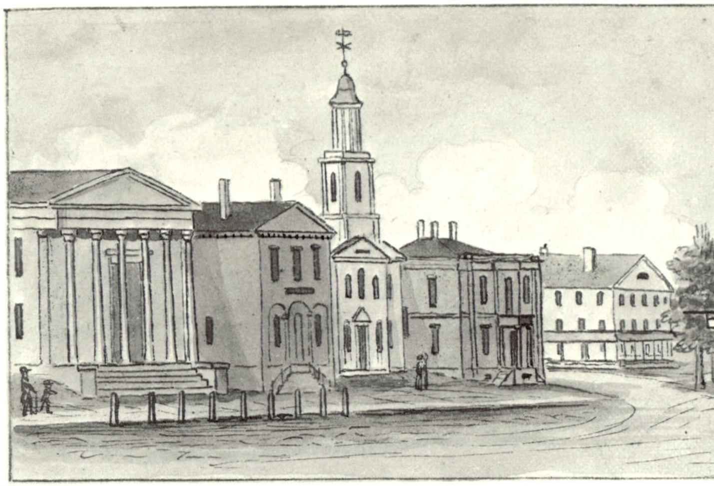

MIDDLETOWN

PUBLIC BUILDINGS IN THE CENTRAL PART

Of the five buildings Barber shows on the west side of Middletown's Main Street (from left to right, the Courthouse, The Middletown Bank, the First Congregational Church, the Customs House, and the Central Hotel) not one remains there. Instead one finds, going north from College Street, The Farmers and Mechanics Bank, a parking lot, the Connecticut Bank and Trust Company, a parking lot, a U.S. Post Office, then, north of Court Street, The Middletown Savings Bank. Across the street is Sears. The Congregational Church (1799) shown by Barber was the church's fourth meeting house in Middletown. After a fashion, it is still to be seen—at the north end of Main Street—where it has been turned around with its back to the street, its ground floor converted to shops. Above the shop windows the church's Palladian window remains, as do large quoins and other original features. The handsome three-tiered spire is gone. The Church's present meeting house, dedicated in 1873, stands on Court Street, a brick neo-Gothic building with a Portland brownstone facade.

JBM

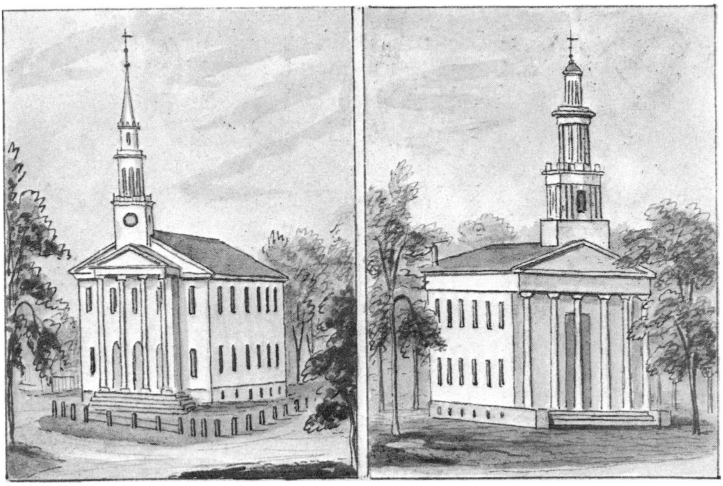

MILFORD

SOUTH VIEW OF THE CONGREGATIONAL CHURCHES

THE MEETING HOUSE on the left, that of the First Church, was built in 1823. To get this view of it, you stand behind the Town Hall on the grass to the west of the river. The other, that of the Second Society and called the Plymouth Church after 1859, was built in 1834. These pictures preceded a larger sketch that shows the two churches on opposite sides of the Wepawaug River with other associated buildings. (The woodcut made from this picture appeared originally in Edward R. Lambert's *History of the Colony of New Haven* [1838] and is reproduced in the W.P.A. history of Milford where you will also find a picture of the Plymouth church as it looked c. 1939). The Second Society was a Great Awakening offshoot which over the years has rejoined, separated, and rejoined the First Church again—the last time in 1926. The Plymouth church was torn down in the early 1950s and replaced by the Plymouth Chapel and Church School, a brick building partly painted white with four columns where six appear here. It is on the island bounded by West Main and North streets and Plymouth Place.

CC

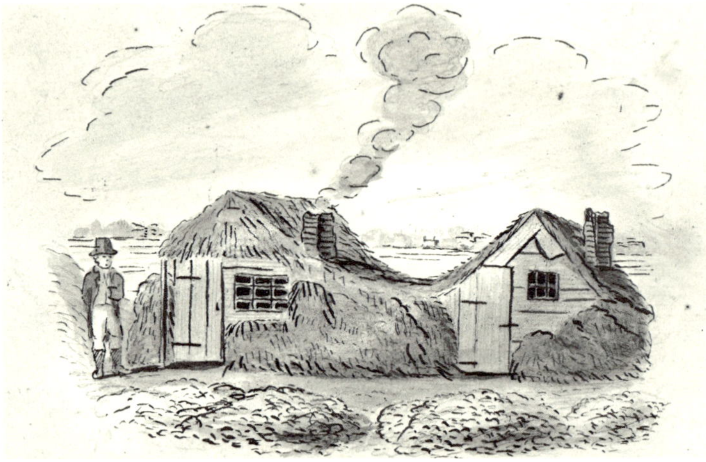

MILFORD

OYSTER HUTS ON MILFORD POINT

64 FOR THOUSANDS OF YEARS oysters were collected at the mouth of the Housatonic River. A major Wepawaug village was located there, and shells many feet deep covered about 23 acres of what became Milford Point. An industry of economic significance since before the middle of the 18th century, oystering, by the 1830s when Barber visited, was a major industry in Milford. Barber reported that about 20 of these seaweed-covered huts were clustered on the spot. In the background is the opposite shore in Stratford. This particular spot cannot be located with any precision. It is probably somewhere near Cedar Beach on Milford Point.

CC

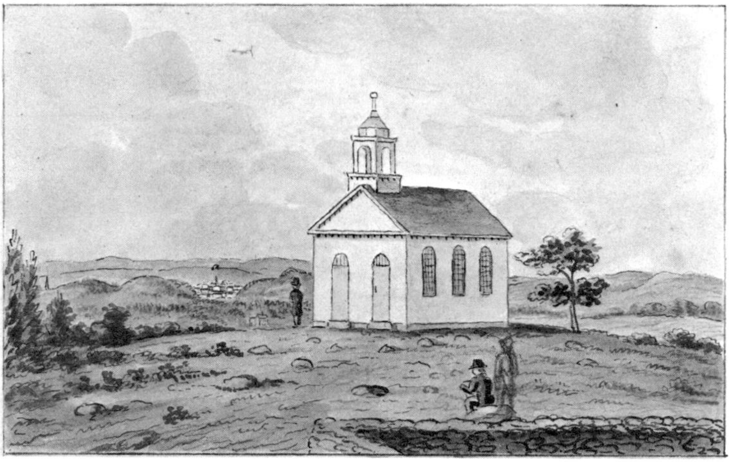

MONTVILLE

SOUTH VIEW OF THE MOHEGAN CHURCH

THE MOHEGAN CHURCH stands on Church Lane, off Route 32 about five miles north of the Montville Town Hall. A sign at the entrance to the lane reads "MOHEGAN, seat of Uncas, the Mohegan sachem friend of the English." Barber remarks, "It is beautifully situated on an eminence commanding a fair view of Norwich at the north [the distant buildings in the picture] and New London at the south. . . . This house is designed for the use of the Mohegans." He adds that "benevolent ladies" in Norwich, Hartford, and New London raised between six and seven hundred dollars for the construction. The wide-open setting Barber shows has given way to residential development. The church itself has been substantially modified: the rounded windows squared; the facade extended forward; and a three-tiered tower with a pointed roof replacing the original columned belfry. Nearby residents, asked about the church, reply, "It's Indian." It is also Congregational, and is still in use.

JBM

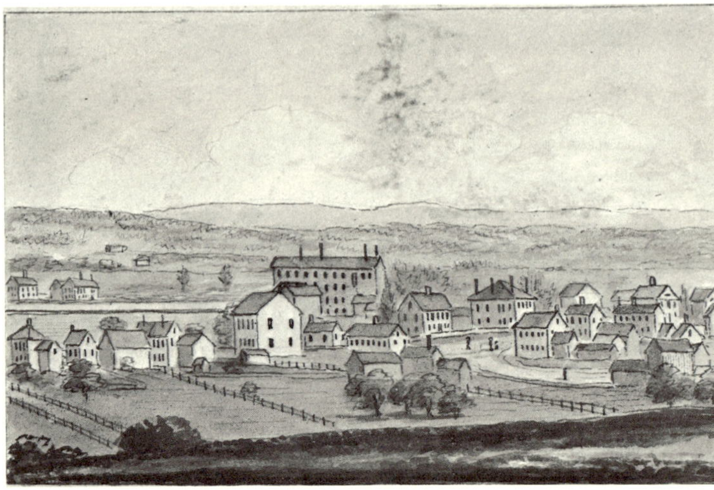

NEW BRITAIN

66 JUST A VERY NEW and small, if "flourishing," manufacturing village when Barber observed it, New Britain has expanded beyond recognition—especially as a result of the maze of late-twentieth-century superhighways that have transformed (if not obliterated) so much of the downtown area of this now good-sized city. Nothing remains but the general terrain; at least from the war monument at the top of Walnut Hill Park the distant hills beyond the Connecticut River look the same. The old, small Methodist church of 1828, located near the center of Barber's engraving, gave way to a massive gray Romanesque structure—the Trinity United Methodist Church that was built in 1889 only a short walk east of the original church. On the southeast corner of Main and Walnut Streets there now stands a fine old brownstone church built in 1865, the South (Congregational) Church with its magnificent steeple and resonating clock chimes. Down on Elm street, where the old North & Stanley brass factory stood, urban renewal and highway development have produced a vista, complete with traffic flow, that (along with much of the rest of downtown New Britain) would numb the senses of John Warner Barber.

ES

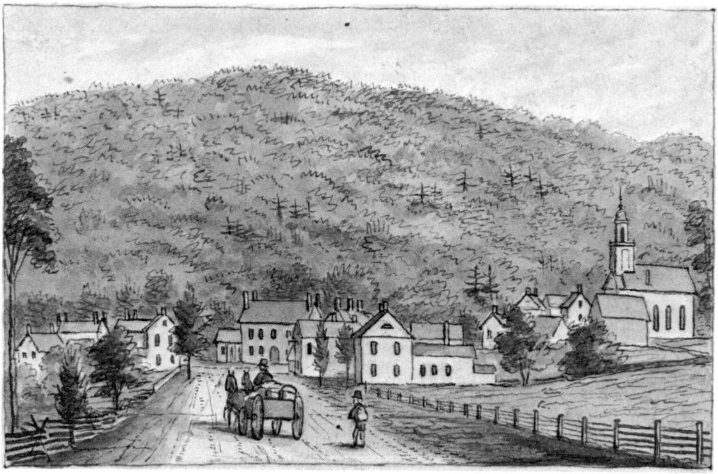

NEW HARTFORD
NORTHERN VIEW

DRIVING SOUTH ON ROUTE 44, the old Albany Turnpike, one descends, as in Barber's time, into a tiny valley through which courses the Farmington River on the east side. The compactness of the town and the surrounding hills remind one of a less grandiose Swiss hamlet. Houses and stores now obscure the open view to the south, though the mountain looms as formidable as ever.

The original town center was a little over two miles south where the oldest Congregational church was located. Settlement shifted to the north, according to Florence Crofut, so that people could be closer to water power and potential mill sites. In 1828 the North Congregational Society was formed and a new brick church, seen to the right and still standing, was built in 1830.

Today, New Hartford has a population of around 5,000. The town suffered heavily from the Great Flood of 1936, which destroyed the Greenwood Dam. Farming is less important than the manufacture of blenders, chairs, and guitars. One mile northeast on Route 219 is the Ski Sundown area, with three chair lifts and four downhill slopes.

ESG

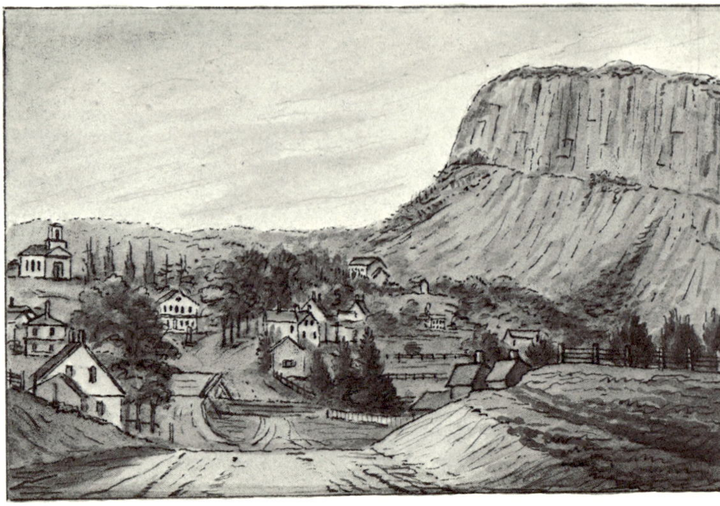

NEW HAVEN
SOUTHWESTERN VIEW OF WEST ROCK AND WESTVILLE

BEGINNING AS A SEPARATE farm village with some manufacturing, Westville was made part of the Township of New Haven in 1868, and finally in 1897 it became part of the city. It was still a rural hamlet when Barber drew this picture showing a view westward along what is now Whalley Avenue shortly before it curves to the right and Fountain Street veers off to the left. Westville Congregational church, now the United Church of Westville, seen in the distance at the far left, was built in 1835 and enlarged in the 1870s. It still stands today on Harrison Street, but the Methodist meetinghouse, shown in the center at the base of West Rock, has not survived. Where only a few structures dotted Barber's landscape, this is today a built-up neighborhood. West Rock, of course, still dominates the scene.

FMS, DFM

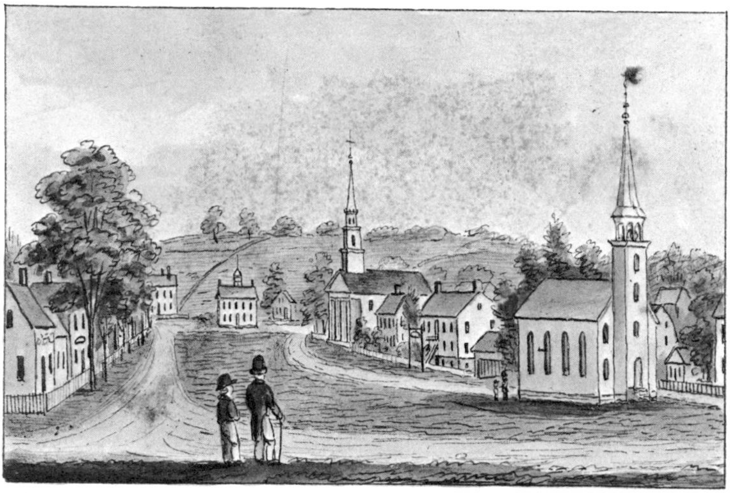

NEW MILFORD

SOUTH VIEW

MUCH OF WHAT APPEARS on the eastern side (right) of Barber's sketch remains. At the head of the green (60 Aspetuck Avenue) stands the Knapp house (1770), now the home of the New Milford Historical Society. The church to the right of this house is still standing, the First Congregational Church (1833), at 42 Main Street.

The house next to the Congregational Church in the view is the Colonel Nathaniel Taylor house (1774), now a private residence. Next to it is the John Taylor house (1827), now occupied by the Litchfield County Times offices.

At 12 Main Street is the Episcopal Church erected in 1837 to replace the church Barber shows. Today it houses the Village Hardware Store.

Most of the buildings on the west side of the green were destroyed in a fire in 1902. The green today is the site of banks, law firms, shops, churches and the public library. The town hall occupies the site of Roger Sherman's residence.

Barber's viewpoint can be reached by Route 202 from the north, Route 67 from the east, or Route 7 from the west. He was looking north on the green where Bank Street goes west and Church Street goes east.

DBE

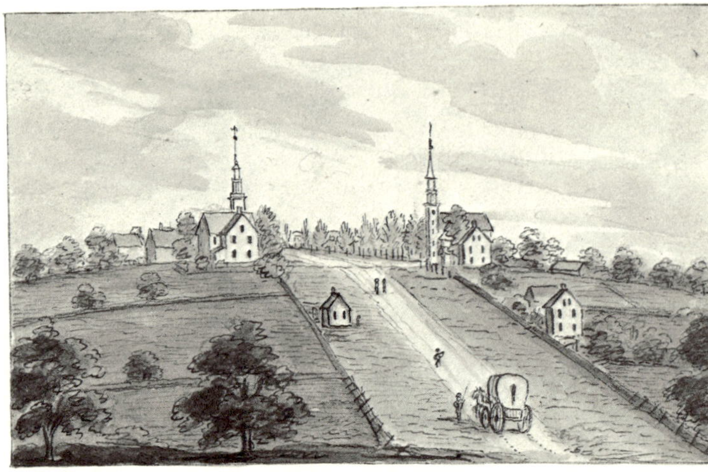

NEWTOWN

SOUTH VIEW

THE TWO CHURCHES are still the main features of hilltop Newtown. The Congregational church shown on the left of Barber's sketch was built in 1808 and is the present church. This was a second structure, replacing a 1720 building (steeple added in 1763) which had been moved slightly west to accommodate the Episcopalians.

The Episcopal church shown on the right was built in 1746 and was replaced by the present stone structure in 1870. Other buildings in Barber's drawing are not identifiable.

Newtown can be reached by Routes I-84 and 6 from the east and west and by Route 25 from the north and south. Barber's viewpoint is on present Route 85, entering town from the south.

DBE

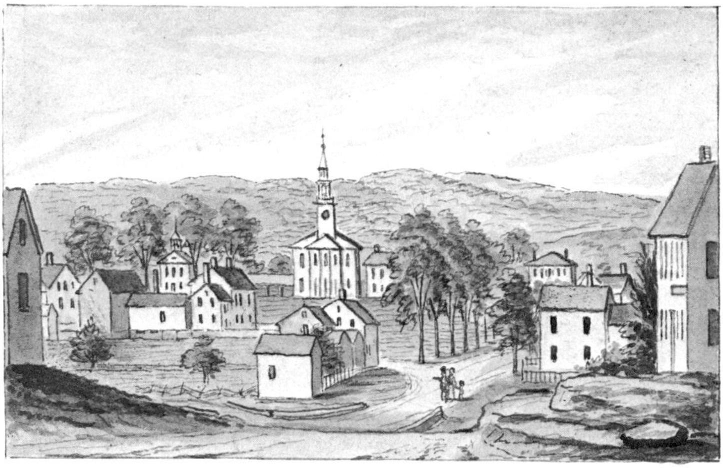

NORFOLK

EAST VIEW OF THE CENTRAL PART

THE CENTRAL FEATURE in Barber's sketch still stands, the Congregational church designed by David Hoadley and built in 1814 to replace the original church built in 1760. The building in the trees to the left of the church was torn down in 1888 to make way for the Battell Chapel designed by J. Cleveland Cady, with windows by Louis Comfort Tiffany. The chapel is part of the Congregational church.

The middle building in the foreground of the church, the Scoville house (1814), remains. It has been a store, shop and library, and is now a medical office and apartments.

The house in the right background was either the Pettibone Tavern (1794), now a condominium, or the White House (c. 1880), built by Joseph Battell and willed to Yale University for its Battell-Stoeckel Summer School of Music.

The house (1806) in the right foreground with the four windows is still a private residence.

Norfolk can be reached by Route 44 east from Canaan or west from Winsted, or by Route 272 north from Torrington. Barber's viewpoint is on Route 44 as one enters from the east.

DBE

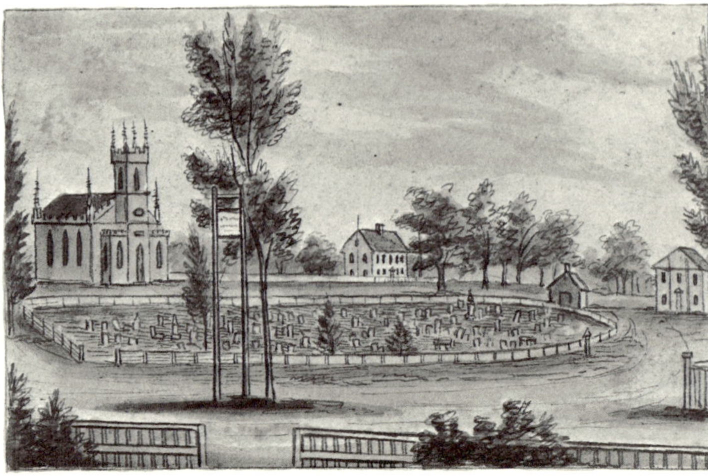

NORTH HAVEN
(CENTRAL PART)

72 THE GREEN, PART OF WHICH is a cemetery, lies east of Church Street (Route 5). Beyond it at the left is St. John's Episcopal Church, facing Trumbull Place, which was built in 1835. A tower was added in 1871, and a religious education building was constructed in 1952. The home of Benjamin Trumbull (1735–1820), Congregational minister from 1760 until his death and author of *History of Connecticut*, published in 1797, is seen in the center. It was erected in 1761. When Barber did this rendering, the Congregational church at the right was in the process of being torn down. Its replacement was located in 1835 several rods toward the west and out of this picture. The present North Haven Congregational church dates from the early 1940s. Exit 12 off Route I-91 leads directly to Church Street.

FMS, DFM

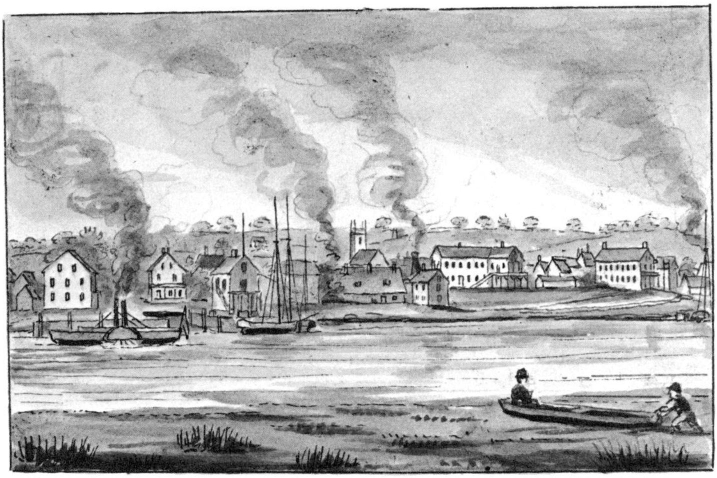

NORWALK

EAST VIEW OF OLD WELL

THIS IS "OLD WELL," so named for a well near what is now the corner of Washington and South Water Streets; in other words, South Norwalk. At the time that Barber drew this sketch, there were six or seven hat factories, three potteries, and a carriage-making shop here. It was also the landing place for the every-other-day steamboat to New York. Straight ahead—looking across the Norwalk River from a rise on the east bank—is the Congregational church, built in 1835. A map made about ten years later, included in Hall's *Norwalk*, identifies the buildings. The dock abutted the present-day Washington Street. Today, at the east end of the Washington Street Bridge, there is a look-out platform at about where Barber stood at the Neptune Boat Club. The view is of the railroad trestle and Norwalk Maritime Center and associated buildings in the redeveloped complex surrounding it.

CC

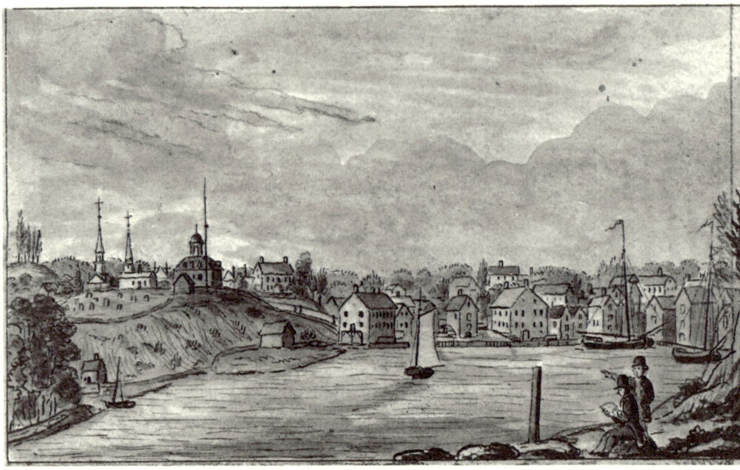

NORWALK

SOUTH VIEW OF THE BOROUGH OF NORWALK

74

THE COMPACT PART of Norwalk was constituted a borough in 1836. Barber described it as "a place of considerable activity and business." It was an entrepot for market boats sailing to New York and supplied a large hinterland. The dome-shaped rise topped with poplars, shown at the extreme right, is Grumman's Hill. A view looking down from Grumman's Hill on the town in 1847 is included in Hall's *Norwalk*. Though Barber calls this a south view—that is, drawn from a point south of town—you are really looking towards the east from a point perhaps one-eighth of a mile west of the river. The Congregational church is on the right with the Episcopal to the left of it and The Green in between. Barber was standing a few hundred yards south of the Methodist Church on West Street. From that point today you see a Congregational church, built in 1924, but looking much like the one sketched here. However, the one Barber drew burned to the ground in 1917. The Town House in the picture was replaced the year he drew this one with a new one which still stands and is used as a museum of town history. Today's view from the same spot includes the triangular common and the block of commercial buildings on Wall Street—none of which date to Barber's era.

CC

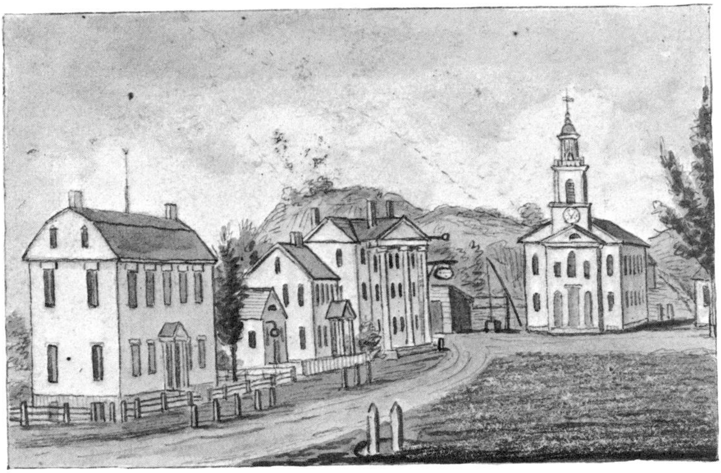

NORWICH

EASTERN VIEW OF THE CENTRAL PART

TWO MILES NORTHWEST of the center of Norwich, the 1801 First Congregational Church still dominates the Town Street approach to the Norwichtown Green. The lawn and trees of the Green extend about 300 feet to the right of the artist's position. A 1971 marker erected by the Society of the Founders of Norwich and the Connecticut Historical Commission describes the busy social and commercial life of the Green during the Revolutionary period, with its taverns, shops, court house, and jail. Now primarily residential, the Green is surrounded by 18th-century houses, a 1783 brick schoolhouse and a 1772 store now serving as a law office. The buildings on the left no longer stand. The church is on West Town Street, six tenths of a mile east of Interstate 395, Exit 82. It is the same distance northwest of the terminus of the Route 2 expressway at Town Street.

BR

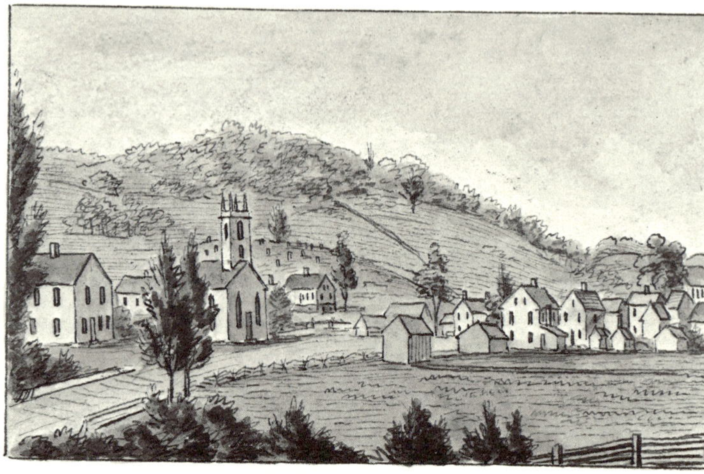

OXFORD

SOUTHEAST VIEW

THE OLD CENTER OF OXFORD, set off from Derby and incorporated in 1798, is located on Route 67 which connects Southbury to New Haven. John Warner Barber placed himself on Oxford Street slightly south of the Green, looking northwest. He was able to include in his view St. Peter's Episcopal Church on the left, built in 1835, and a portion of the Congregational church on the extreme right constructed in 1795. According to Barber, the hill in the background was called "Governor's Hill" because its owner was a man of lordly airs who frequently went to court in defense of "his real or imaginary rights."

The scene has changed but would be still recognizable to a mid-nineteenth century resident revisiting the town. The wooden bridge over Little River has been replaced and the road widened. St. Peter's Church retains its Gothic windows, but has lost its steeple. The Congregational church which originally had a square tower (seen in Barber's pencil sketch but not the ink wash) has been extensively remodeled in the Greek Revival style and its interior completely renovated. The eighteenth and nineteenth century houses along Oxford Street seen in the right of Barber's view have been restored.

CPB

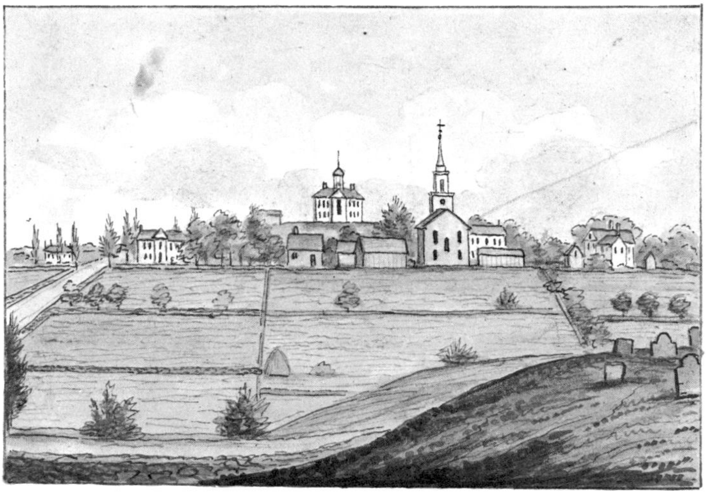

PLAINFIELD

WESTERN VIEW

POSITIONING HIMSELF to the west of the village, Barber selected a dramatic point from which to draw the town center. In the right foreground is a corner of a cemetery that is now, understandably, far more extensive. Rectangular fields outlined by substantial stone walls characteristic of eastern Connecticut form the middle ground of the view. In the distance, along a ridge running from north to south, is a row of buildings that includes the stone Congregational church designed by Ithiel Town and completed in 1818. At the peak of the hill stands the principal building, a stone structure completed in 1825, of the Plainfield Academy, a preparatory school incorporated in 1784 which soon developed a national reputation for excellence. The town now can no longer claim the educational distinction of a famous academy, but its fine stone church is now undergoing restoration. The view of the center of the town from the west still gives the visitor a pleasing vista combining open fields and a line of old structures.

CPB

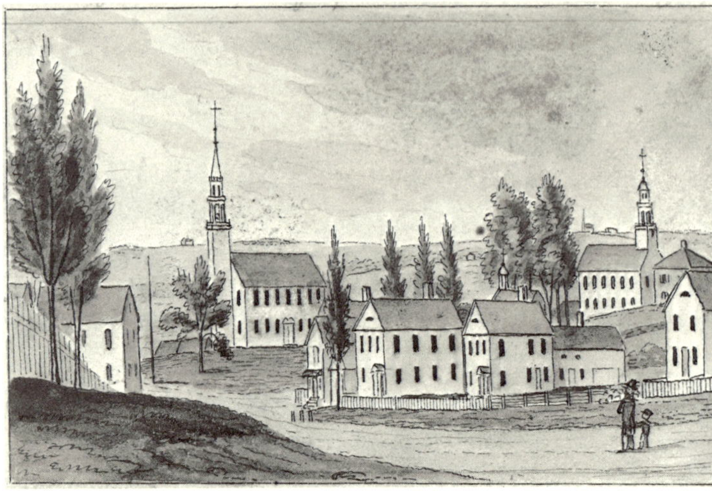

PLYMOUTH

EAST VIEW OF THE

CENTRAL PART OF PLYMOUTH

IN THE CENTER OF THIS DRAWING is the Plymouth Congregational church, the second of three on the same foundation. It was built in 1792 and replaced in 1837 soon after Barber visited the site. At the time the church was replaced, the new structure was turned ninety degrees so that today it faces east (towards Park Street) rather than south (towards Route 6).

To the right is the old St. Peter's Episcopal church which was built in 1796 and destroyed by fire in 1915. In that year the present St. Peter's, built of fireproof native stone, was constructed just across the green from the Congregational church. A bronze plaque on a boulder at the northeast corner of the green marks the site of the old St. Peter's. Just to the left of the Episcopal spire, on a hilltop far to the northwest, is the church of Northfield Parish in the southeast corner of Litchfield.

In the center of the view one can see a small cupola nestled near the trees. It rests atop the Stoughton Building that sits next to the Congregational church today. The building on the far right was razed and on its site stands the Plymouth public library.

CC

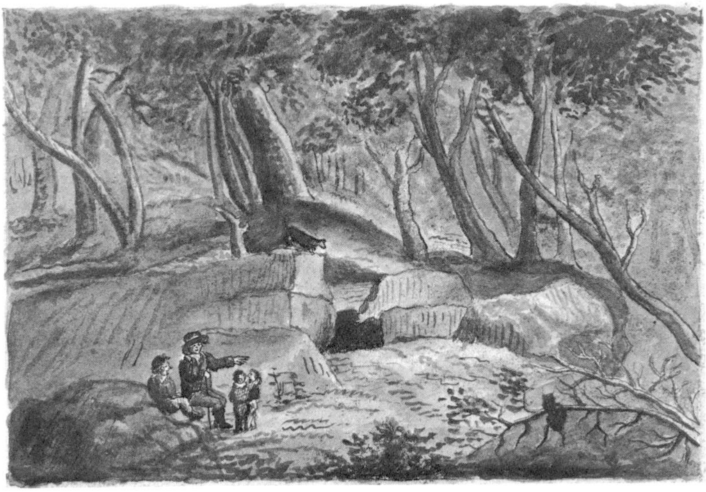

POMFRET

PUTNAM'S CAVE OR WOLF DEN

DURING THE NINETEENTH CENTURY, the story of Israel Putnam's slaying of a predatory wolf in 1743 was almost as well known as the legend of the Charter Oak. The old wolf preyed upon the stock of area farms successfully evading area hunters determined to rid themselves of the nuisance. Finally, a team of five men agreed to pursue the wolf until he could be trapped. At last the beast took refuge in a remote cave where all efforts to dispatch the animal failed. After removing his coat, Putnam was lowered into the cave with a rope. He entered the dark pit with a blazing torch only to be pulled out again. Back he went and this time he shot and killed the wolf.

The story was told and retold because it seemed to presage Putnam's courage and leadership in the Revolution. For his text, Barber here simply quotes from David Humphreys' biography. In his picture of the wolf den, which was taken from a sketch by "Mr. Fisher" (possibly Alvan Fisher), a father is shown pointing to the opening in the cave presumably passing the story on to his children. The site of the cave is now located on state land in Wolf Den Park on Route 44, a short walk from the parking lot.

CPB

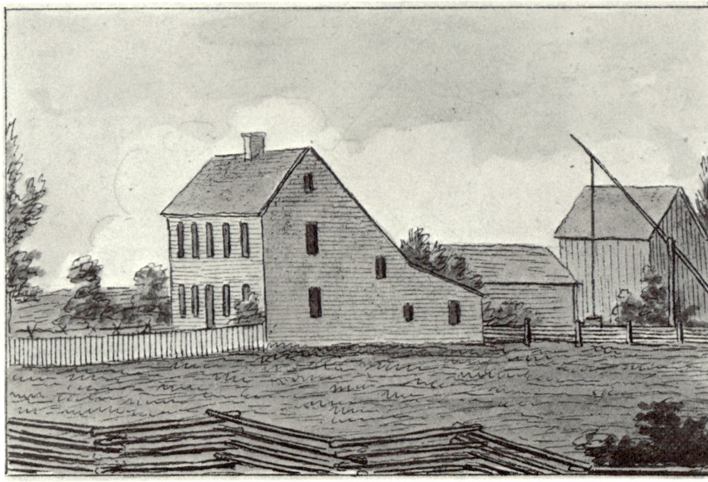

REDDING: NORTH VIEW OF HOUSE IN REDDING, FORMERLY GEN. PUTNAM'S HEADQUARTERS

80 THIS IS THE HOUSE that local legend—which we have no reason to challenge—tells us was used by Israel Putnam as his headquarters when his troops were bivouacked in Redding in 1778. Crowfut's statement that "opinions vary regarding the situation of Putnam's headquarters" probably grows out of the use of different names for the road which went past it. Barber's Norwalk and Danbury Road is either the present day Umpawaug Hill or Simpaug Turnpike. Local authority locates the site at the junction of Topstone Road on the west side of Umpawaug. It is probable that the zig-zag fence runs along the road, so Barber was looking west at the sunset as he drew this picture. If you were to stand on the same spot today, your view would show a house built probably in the early 19th century that is clearly not the one that Barber drew. The evidence still leaves us wondering where the Putnam headquarters was.

CC

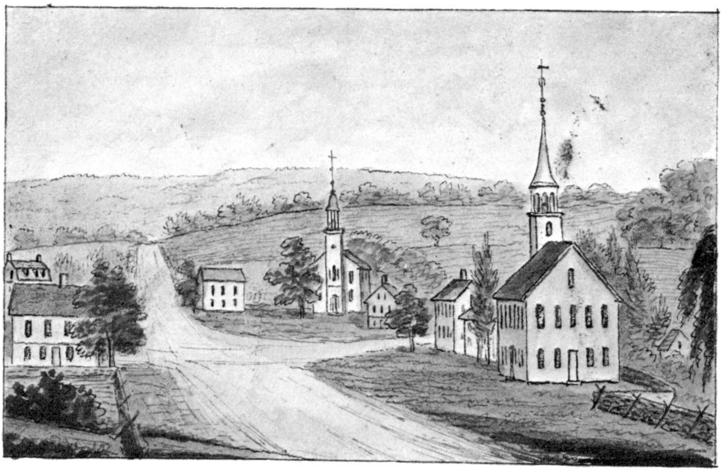

ROXBURY

NORTHEASTERN VIEW

ROXBURY, set off from Woodbury in 1743 and incorporated as a town in 1796, is one of those rural communities which was spared the heavy hand of industrialization. The town center retains a great deal of the appearance that greeted John Warner Barber in the mid-1830s, although changing circumstances have led residents to modify, reorient, and, occasionally, to replace the buildings seen in the ink wash. Christ Church, the Episcopal church built in 1807 and shown in the center of the picture, now faces west. Its exterior has been Gothicized, possibly in the 1860s when the church was shifted on its axis. The Congregational church seen on the right and two buildings on the left no longer stand. A new Congregational church was constructed a few miles away in 1838. The gabled and gambrel houses shown on the left have been altered over the years, but are also still standing.

CPB

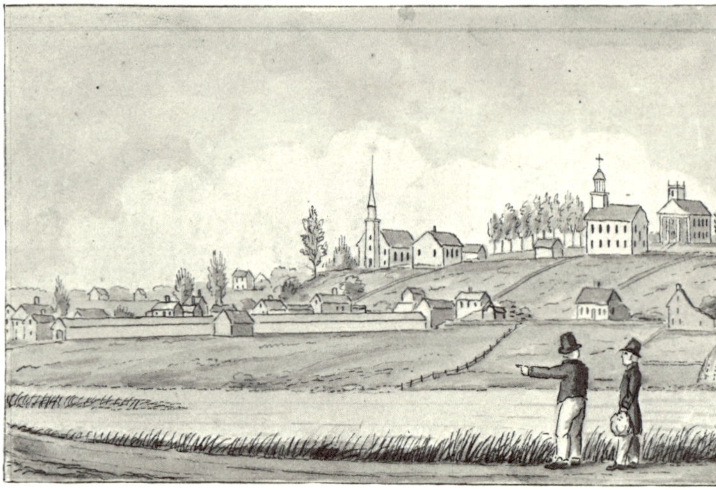

ESSEX

NORTHEAST VIEW OF THE BOROUGH OF ESSEX, SAYBROOK

NORTHEAST VIEW of the Borough of Essex, Saybrook no longer exits. In the first place, Essex is a flourishing village and no longer needs Saybrook's support. And Barber's view is obliterated by hundreds of trees and scores of houses. The two long rope walk buildings are gone but there is an excellent painting of them in the Essex Historical Society, housed in Hills Academy building which was constructed in 1832. Just to the right are located the Roman Catholic church and next to it the Baptist church. Barber took some artistic license in his picture, for the Methodist church is a bit further to the south than illustrated. It has been completely rebuilt as a private home, part of the steeple having been turned into a sun room. The Episcopal church that is illustrated was torn down long ago and a stone church built on Essex Main Street. Between Barber's Episcopal and Methodist churches is now located the Congregational church. Just to the left on the east and down the hill is Essex Main Street.

JMKD

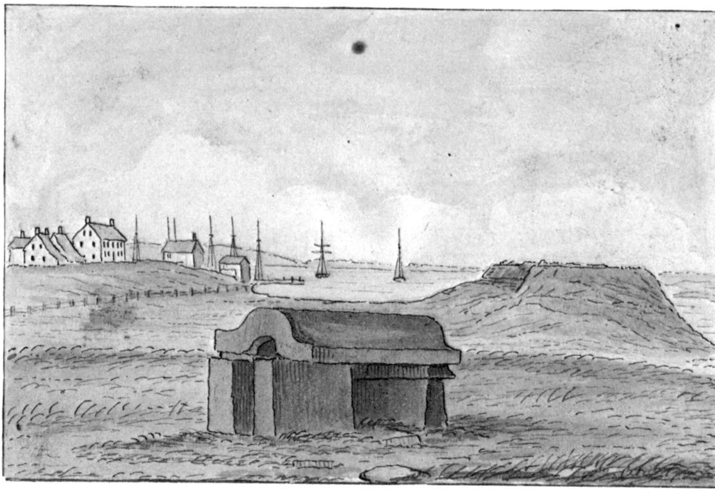

OLD SAYBROOK

SOUTH VIEW OF

LADY FENWICK'S MONUMENT

LADY FENWICK'S GRAVE and monument were moved November 23, 1870 from the site of Fort Saybrook to Cypress Cemetery located about four hundred yards to the north and across College Street. Just north of the cemetery College Street becomes Saybrook Main Street. The move was made because the Connecticut Valley Railroad was scheduled to be extended to Saybrook Point to what is now known as Monument Park. Much dirt was moved so that a turntable for the railroad could be installed. The foundation for the turntable can be seen which is approximately where Lady Fenwick's grave was located originally. Next to Cypress Cemetery is a monument marking the place where Yale College was founded.

JMKD

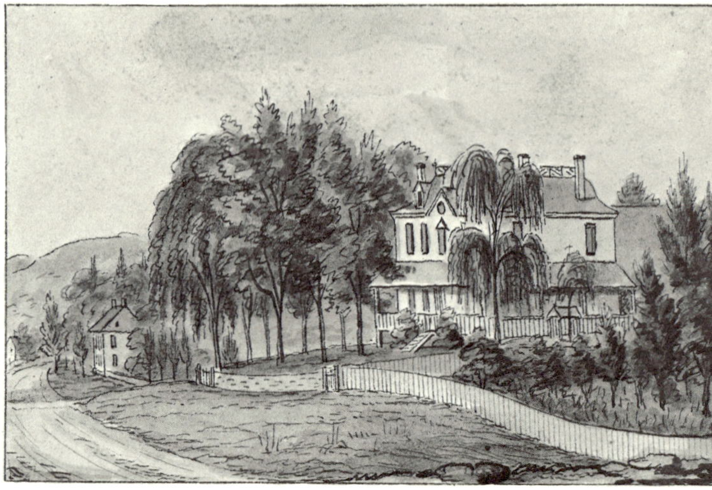

SHARON

SOUTH VIEW OF GOV. SMITH'S HOUSE

84 SHARON'S BROAD, TREE-LINED Main Street is well worth a trip to the north-west corner of the state. Among the many handsome houses there, the jewel in the crown is the Smith mansion, begun in 1757 by Dr. Simeon Smith and later the home of Connecticut's Governor John Cotton Smith.

This large square stone-and-brick structure, generally gray shading to pale blues and pinks, with an ell at the back, is set in well-kept grounds shaded by large trees, among which a magnificent copper beech is particularly notable. The landscaping includes a flower garden bordered by a high hedge, a large stylish greenhouse, a paddock, a tennis court, a rose garden, and much more.

The covered veranda shown in Barber's view has been removed, being replaced by an open brick porch from which stairs curve gracefully down to ground level on either side. The picket fence is gone, too, the street-front being edged by a low stone wall backed by shrubs, mostly lilacs. The front-yard rose garden with its central figurine is set within a wooden enclosure painted white to match the mansion's trim, which includes the frames of the large twelve-over-twelve windows and the Chippendale-style railing of the hip roof, visible in Barber's view.

JBM

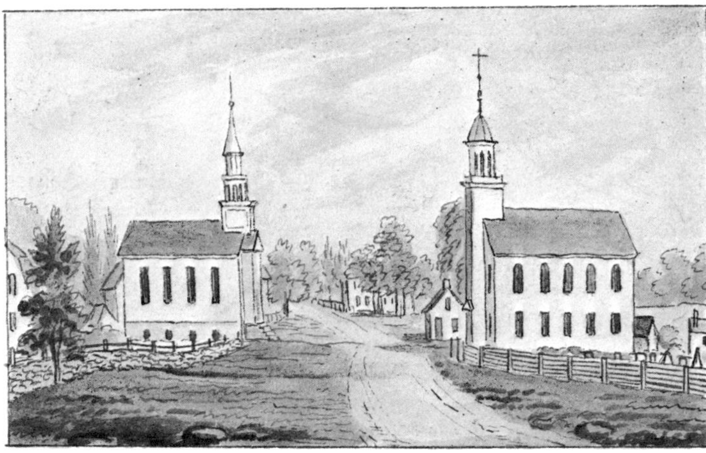

SHELTON: SOUTH VIEW OF THE EPISCOPAL AND CONGREGATIONAL CHURCHES IN HUNTINGTON

HUNTINGTON, NAMED AFTER Governor Samuel Huntington, changed its name in 1919 to Shelton to honor its leading capitalist, a descendant of the primary founder of the town.

The two churches shown here appear to look today as they do in the sketch, but they are not the same. St. Paul's Episcopal, on the right or east, is much obscured by a row of large hemlocks that run between Church Road, also Route 108, and Old Huntington Cemetery. The Congregational church is shielded by a row of maples. Though the present church is shaped like the one in the picture, with a virtually identical spire, it is not the same. The present church—the fourth near this site—was built in 1892 to replace one built shortly after 1832 when an earlier one burned down. Barber notes that the one in the sketch was "recently erected."

The small house behind St. Paul's is no longer there, but Huntington green stretches northerly beyond the church. At the north end of the green today stands the house of Huntington's first minister, but it doesn't look like the one in this sketch, built in 1735, nor is the site just right. The one shown here was probably on a site now occupied by a United Illuminating Company relay station.

CC

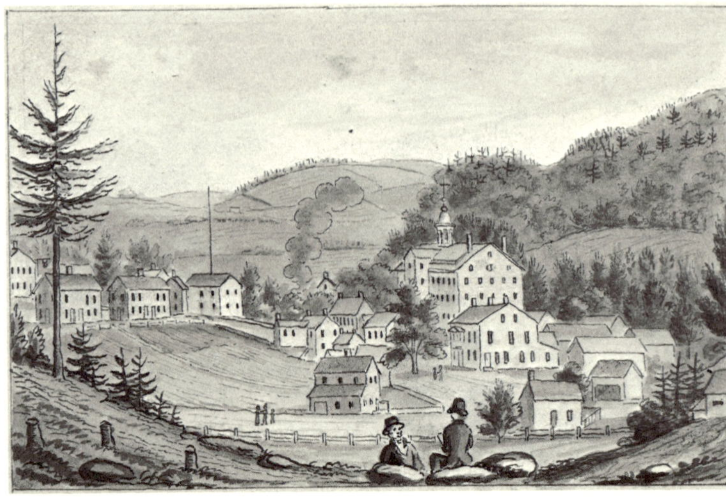

SIMSBURY

SOUTH VIEW OF TARIFFVILLE

86 THE OLD CARPET MILL that dominates Barber's sketch of Tariffville is barely visible from the southern heights because of the intervening concentration of houses. Beyond the mill the Farmington River that provided waterpower flows through the awesome Tariffville gorge. America's first carpet factory was built in 1825 by three Hartford entrepreneurs. Both the company and the village were named after the tariff passed by Congress on imported carpets in 1824. In 1840 it was taken over by the Thompsonville Manufacturing Company and employed nearly 200 men. Fire destroyed the mill and part of the village in 1867. Only four of the workers' homes in the Greek Revival style survived. In 1881 the Hartford Silk Company occupied the mill for a short time. Since then a succession of hardware and textile firms have used it, but at present it stands vacant. Today, Tariffville, only a few miles south of Newgate on Route 187 from Bloomfield, hardly fits Barber's description of "flourishing."

ESG

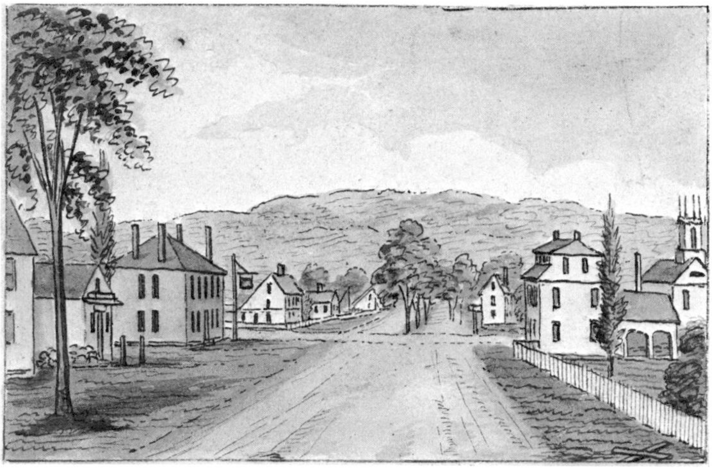

SOMERS

WEST VIEW

ALTHOUGH THE CROSSROADS that appear in Barber's sketch are readily identifiable there is little else that remains.

The building on the left with the four chimneys, the Somers Inn, has continued over the years as a hostelry and restaurant.

The Methodist church (1834), shown at the right, was moved from South Road to Main Street later. It was closed in 1900, damaged by fire in 1913, and restored as Piedmont Hall by the R. H. Kibbe family for use as a public hall. In 1937 the hall was donated to the Somers Congregational church. In 1948 it was purchased by a private party and operated as a theatre. It was donated to the town later and moved westward to a new foundation where it became the public library. The Congregational church (1842) on Main Street was not built until after Barber's sketch.

Somers can be reached by Route 190 from the east and west (Main Street) and by Route 80 from the north and south. Barber's viewpoint was on Main Street just west of the crossing of the two routes.

DBE

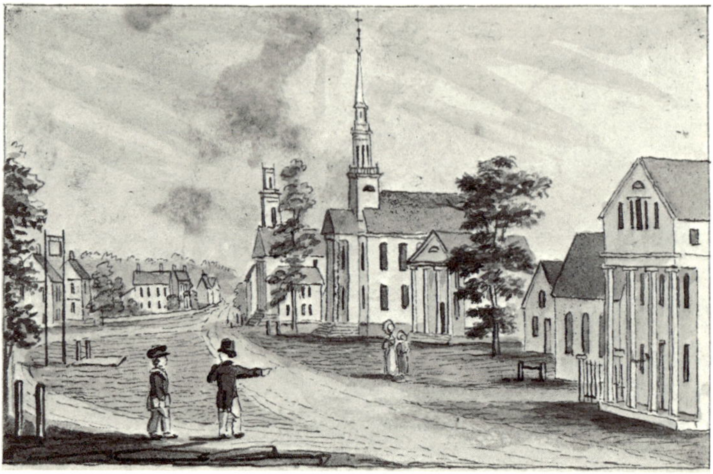

SOUTHINGTON

SOUTH VIEW

(CENTRAL PART)

THE FIRST CONGREGATIONAL CHURCH Meeting House still dominates the skyline of Southington as it did more than a century and a half ago. Aside from this handsome building, the center of town bears little resemblance to that of the original Barber picture. Few old buildings remain now: the Baptist church is gone; a new Town Hall, built in 1941, is located across Academy Street just south of the Congregational church; and the Episcopal church, while still on Main Street, has moved south of Berlin Avenue, the road that Barber has turning off to the East between the old Post Office and the original Episcopal Church building. A small town park still survives across Main Street from the Congregational Church, but most of the busy highway through this old part of Southington is now lined with an assortment of one or two-story commercial buildings. Just north of the town center Main Street (State Route 10) becomes Queen Street, and this "Old College Highway" becomes a new shopping-mall thoroughfare that leads to Interstate Route 84 and then north to Plainville and Farmington.

ES

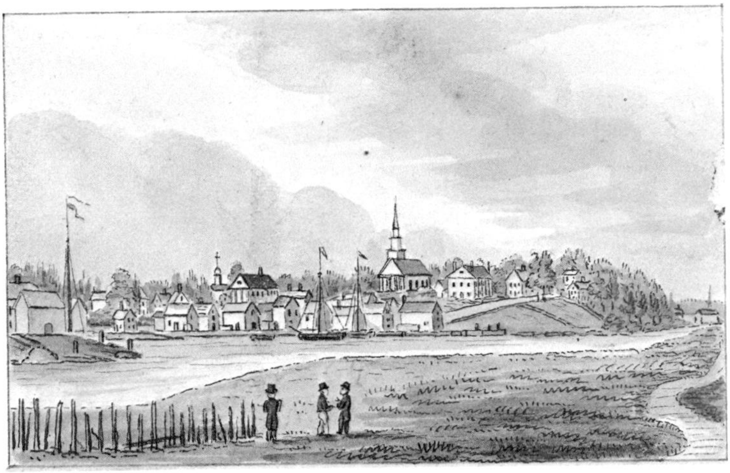

FAIRFIELD

SOUTH VIEW OF THE BOROUGH OF SOUTHPORT

BARBER SKETCHED SOUTHPORT HARBOR at the village's most vital moment in its economic development. Ten years before he drew this picture the newly established borough contained only about twenty buildings, but in 1835 it had grown to sixty or seventy, and was the export point for "a considerably extensive and fertile back country." On the extreme right of the sketch is a flour mill, behind which rises the spire of the Episcopal church in Fairfield. The mill stood on Herdsman's Island in the river on what is now Harbor Road. The Trinity Episcopal chapel, built in 1835, stands on the rise in the center, at the summit of Rose Hill. To the left is the Mill River branch of the Connecticut Bank, later the Southport National Bank. To the left is the spire-topped Southport Academy, built in 1828. The church burned down in 1854, and was rebuilt on a site about a half mile east. The Academy building was sold in 1855, moved slightly and, without its cupola, continues as a residence at 95 Main Street. Barber was standing on the levee that bounds the golf course of the Country Club of Fairfield somewhat down stream from hole four (par 3).

CC

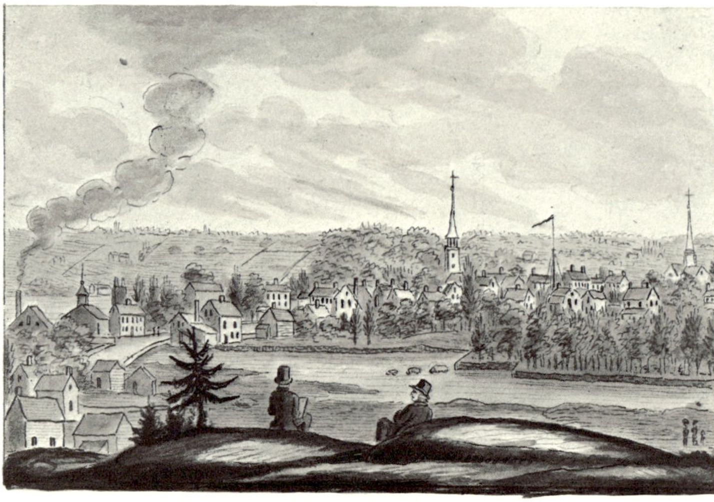

STAMFORD

SOUTH VIEW OF THE BOROUGH OF STAMFORD

90 SIXTY YEARS AGO a historian of Stamford wrote: "Everywhere is change. The spirits of the departed should they wander over the town they came to love, would find little to recall it to their memory." Barber's view of the Borough of Stamford looking across Mill River to the northeast is now a very distant memory. In the middle of the view on Bank Street stood the First Congregational Church, the fourth on that site, which was replaced in 1858. In 1911 the present church was built on Prospect and Bedford Streets. The Episcopal Church seen on the right of the image was replaced in 1842–43 and that building was in turn destroyed by fire in 1890 and replaced. The mast in the center of the picture is from a sloop being towed up the town canal constructed in 1833 but rendered obsolete by the coming of the railroad in 1848 and then gradually filled in after 1868. The smoke pouring from the chimney was from an iron foundry that manufactured stoves. Long a manufacturing center, the Stamford skyline is today shaped not by church spires but by towers occupied by Fortune 500 companies.

CPB

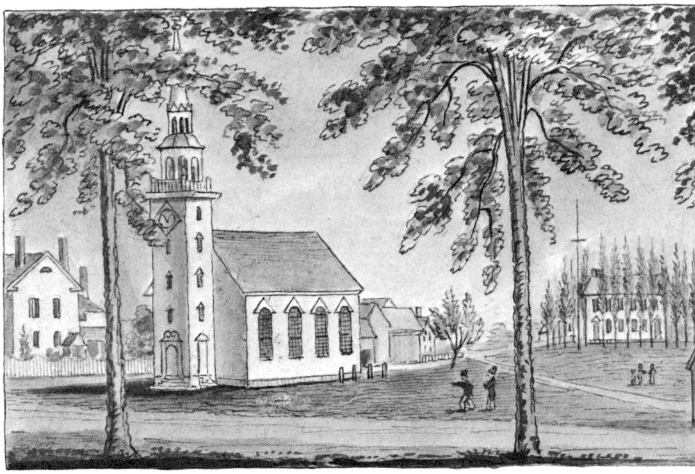

STRATFORD

SOUTHWEST VIEW OF THE EPISCOPAL CHURCH

CONNECTICUT EPISCOPALIANISM was born in Stratford in 1706, and the present church there is only the third since the first was built in 1723. The Episcopal church in Barber's view, built in 1743, was torn down in 1858. A rooster weathercock, obscured by leaves in the sketch, was preserved and sits again on top of the steeple. One can still view the church along Main Street, but the road behind the church, known as King's Highway in the colonial era, no longer exists.

Lovejoy's Tavern, the building seen to the left, was moved in 1864, used as a funeral home in the 20th century, and torn down in 1976 to be replaced with a used car lot. The old Academy built in 1805, seen on the right, was also moved and used as a Baptist church before it was demolished in the 1930s. The hill where it stood was known as Watch Hill, then Meeting House Hill, and Academy Hill from 1805 to the present.

CC

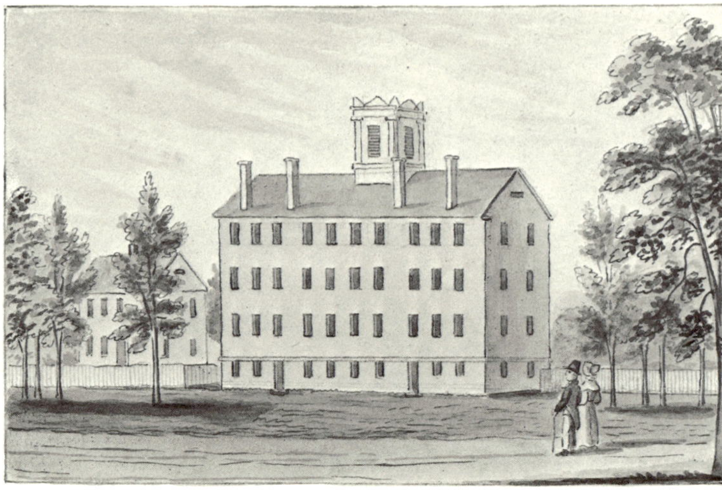

SUFFIELD

CONNECTICUT LITERARY INSTITUTION

92 THE CONNECTICUT LITERARY INSTITUTION, now called the Suffield Academy, is located at Main Street, west of the Green, Route 75, Suffield. The building, pictured by Barber, was built and dedicated in 1834 and served for more than sixty years before it was demolished.

The Connecticut Literary Institution was founded under the patronage of the Connecticut Baptist Education Society in 1823. The school served as the only source for higher-education in the town until the 1870s with the introduction of public high schools. A women's department was introduced in 1843 and additional buildings were added in 1845 and 1851. As the Suffield Academy it is in flourishing condition and is highly rated among this country's preparatory schools. The fee of "1 dol.25cts. per week" for the steward who furnishes board including washing, as stated by Barber, no longer prevails.

CLR

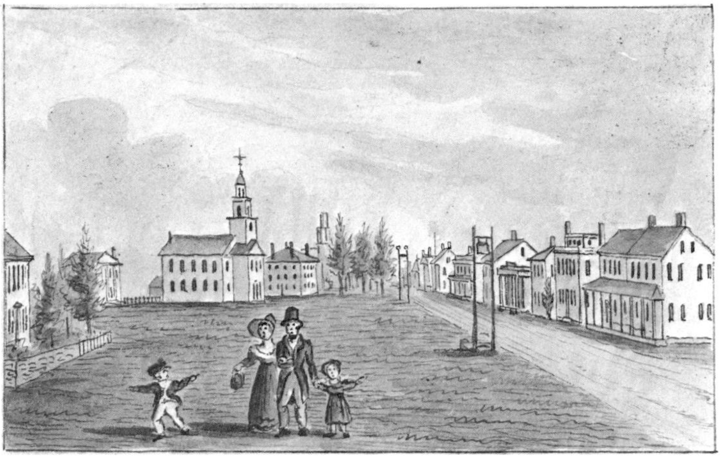

THOMPSON
SOUTH VIEW
(CENTRAL PART)

THE PRESENT CONGREGATIONAL CHURCH (1856), which lost its tower in a fire in 1987, is situated directly across from the Congregational church shown in Barber's sketch.

A house to the left of the first church was razed some years ago, and the site is now occupied by the post office. The house shown to the right of the church dates from the late 1700s, is in the Federalist style, and is still standing.

The fourth building from the right, with columns, was the Thompson Bank. It was dismantled, moved and rebuilt at Old Sturbridge Village. The fifth building may have been the old brick schoolhouse and the sixth the Vernon Stiles Inn, where Lafayette stayed on a post-Revolutionary War visit to America. The present Congregational church stands in this area.

The center of Thompson shown in Barber's sketch is at the intersection of Routes 193 and 200 and can also be reached via Exit 99 of the Connecticut Turnpike (I-395). Barber's viewpoint is on Route 193, looking north toward the center.

DBE

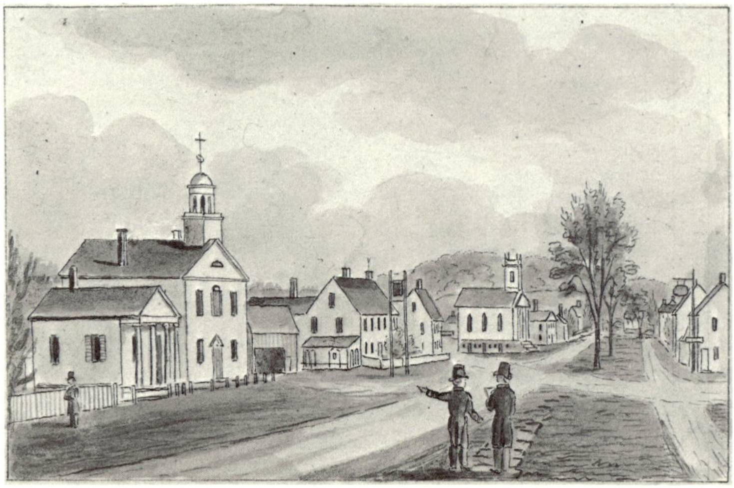

TOLLAND

SOUTH VIEW OF THE CENTRAL PART

94 TOLLAND IS ON ROUTE 74 and can be reached by taking Exit 69 off the Interstate 84, the country is rolling and the area is very scenic. Two of the buildings in Barber's view, looking north along the village green, still stand: the Tolland County Bank Building, now the Board of Education, and the former County Court House.

The present-day Tolland area was first purchased from the Indians by residents of Windsor in 1636, but it was not until 1713 in the southern portion and 1719 in the northern portion that a Windsor committee laid out and assigned sections to Windsor taxpayers. Most of the early settlers were an overflow from Windsor.

CLR

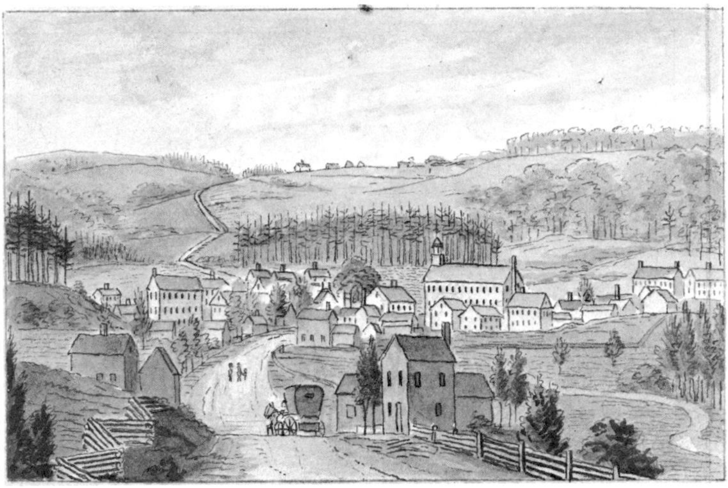

TORRINGTON

NORTHEAST VIEW OF WOLCOTTVILLE

SETTLED IN THE 1740s, Torrington was principally an agricultural town until the establishment of a woolen mill in 1802 owned by Governor Oliver Wolcott after whom the village of Wolcottville was named. By 1835, when Barber visited the place, the village consisted of some 40 dwellings, several stores, a Congregational church, a three-story brick building that served as a house of worship for several denominations and as an academy, and the woolen factory. Barber could not include the church in his view; the brick building is seen to the left and the factory, with its bell tower, appears to the right of the picture. Barber notes that a factory for the manufacture of brass kettles, the first to use the battery process, was under construction.

None of the buildings in Barber's view remain standing. The last survivor, the three-story brick structure, was taken down in the 1940s. Today, traffic flows along commercial East Main Street westward to Litchfield (on Route 25), over the east branch of the Naugatuck river, past Torrington Sash and Door Company which now dominates the scene. Only the river and the shape of the distant hills remind us of the Wolcottville that once was.

CPB

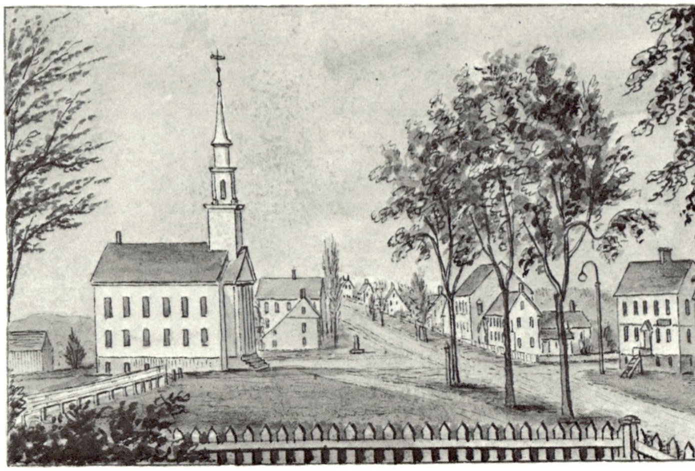

WALLINGFORD

(CENTRAL PART)

96 LOOKING NORTH ON WHAT is now Main Street at the intersection of Center Street, one sees the First Congregational church on the left, the First Baptist church just beyond it, and St. Paul's Episcopal church across the street in the building without a chimney. The artist did not identify the other structures, which appear to be residences. Since Barber's day everything has changed at this location, which is about midway between Route I-91 and the Wilbur Cross Parkway (Route 15). All three congregations erected new houses of worship at the same places as the old ones, in 1868, 1870, and 1868 respectively, all in the Gothic Revival style. St. Paul's was enlarged in 1890, the Post Office today stands on the southwest corner of the intersection, and along the streets everywhere else there are stores.

FMS, DFM

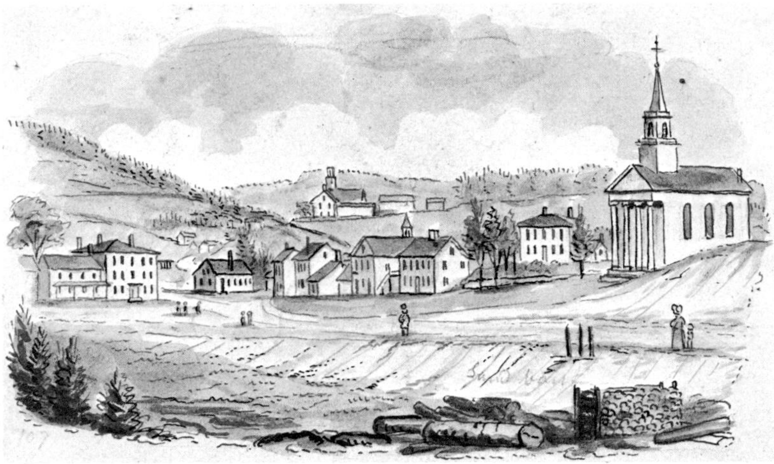

WARREN

EAST VIEW OF CENTRAL PART

JOHN WARNER BARBER probably visited Warren on one of his trips to Litchfield County in the Fall of 1835 when he made a sketch and later an ink wash. Barber chose to present his brief entry on Warren without an engraved view. Thus the ink wash shown here is an unpublished view of the town. Barber noted that the town was agricultural and that its population had declined between 1800 and 1830.

The only surviving features depicted in Barber's view of Warren are the church and the hill on which it sits. All other buildings have been either removed or replaced with modern structures. Details of the church have been modified since Barber's visit, though the basic proportions remain intact.

CPB

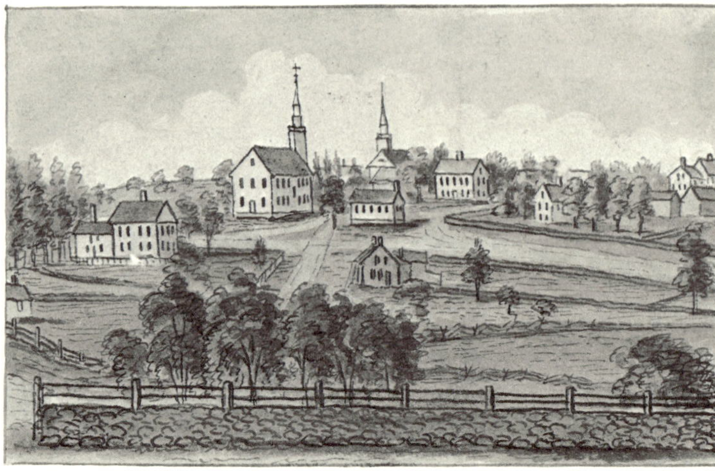

WATERTOWN

NORTHEASTERN VIEW

98

BARBER SKETCHED THE CENTER OF WATERTOWN looking in a southwesterly direction. The First Congregational Church built in 1772, the second meeting house in Watertown, is seen on the left and Christ Episcopal Church, built in 1794, is on the right. The building to the right of the Episcopal Church is the parsonage built for the Rev. John Trumbull which still stands. The structure in front of the Episcopal Church was a schoolhouse that reportedly was moved across town and raised upon a brick foundation to form a two-story building. Both churches were themselves replaced later in the nineteenth century. A new Congregational Church was built up on a hill just a few rods west of the earlier building in 1840 and the Episcopal Church was constructed further south on the Green in 1855. The Episcopal church of 1855 served the community until 1923 when it was taken down and the present church built on the old foundation. The handsome Congregational church which now faces a Soldier's Monument overlooking Main Street is well preserved and is flanked on one side by the old town hall now used for town offices and the historical society and, on the other, by the Trumbull house. The present Town Hall built in 1894 stands on the site of the earlier Congregational church.

CPB

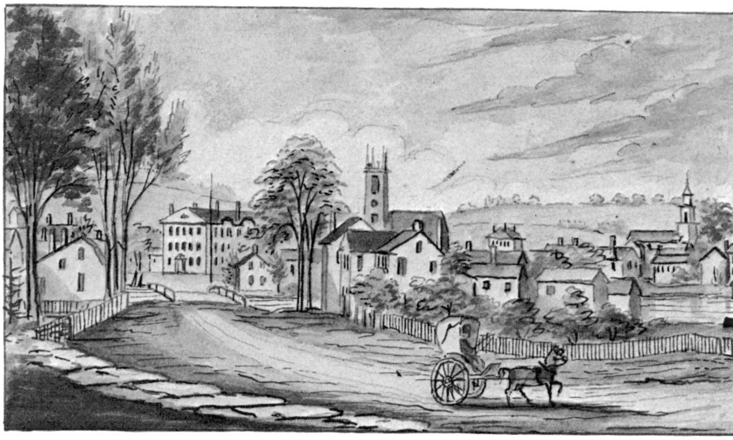

WATERTOWN
SOUTHERN VIEW
(CENTRAL PART)

BARBER CHOSE NOT TO USE THIS VIEW of Watertown in his book; thus we do not have his description to aid us in identifying the buildings. He appears to have positioned himself to the southeast of the Green looking towards what is called Nova Scotia Hill in his book, but which was identified as Scott's Mountain in an earlier account. He apparently stood at what is now the intersection of Porter Street and Echo Lake Road facing a small bridge that spanned Steele Brook. The spire on the left is Christ Episcopal church built in 1794 and the Congregational church built in 1772 is seen on the right, both of which were later replaced and relocated. The three-story structure seen in the center has not been identified.

CPB

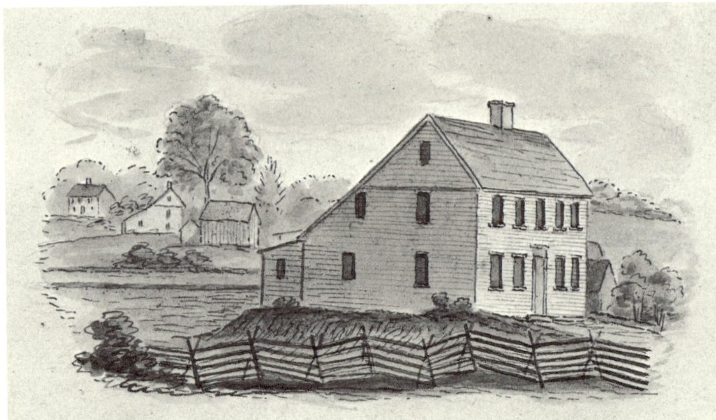

WATERTOWN

NORTH VIEW OF THE TRUMBULL HOUSE

THE PRESTIGE OF JUDGE JOHN TRUMBULL (1750–1831), once considered the most important American poet of the Revolution, has dimmed somewhat since John Warner Barber visited Watertown in 1835. To Barber, Trumbull was a figure of great significance whose modest birthplace deserved a place in his guide to Connecticut history and towns. The first home of the Rev. John Trumbull (1715–1787), the first minister of the Watertown Congregational church, was a saltbox built around 1739, the year Trumbull was ordained. It stood about a half mile south of the Congregational church on the east side of Main Street on the Waterbury road. A watering trough with a dedicatory plaque was placed near the site by the Sarah Whitman Trumbull chapter of the D.A.R. in 1905 sometime after the house was demolished. The fountain itself was later reduced in size when Main Street was widened, leaving only the plaque to mark the spot of the house. In 1772 the Rev. John Trumbull built a more elaborate house close to the second Congregational church which still stands.

CPB

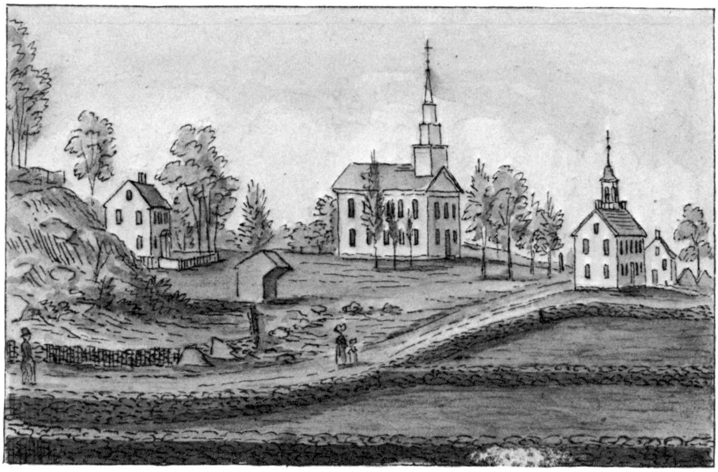

EASTON: SOUTHWESTERN VIEW OF THE CONGREGATIONAL CHURCH AND ACADEMY IN WESTON

THIS VIEW IS OF THE Congregational church in Easton, set off from Weston as a separate town in 1845, and the Staples Academy, built with funds donated by Samuel Staples. The church was built in 1835; the Academy in 1796. The Academy, a distinguished educational institution, continued for about a century, closed for a couple of years and reopened as a public school, and after 1931, was used as a parish hall by the church. If you stand just a few yards west of the Academy driveway on Westport Road (Route 136) you will see this view almost exactly as Barber did. Two of the sugar maples in front of the church still stand (two others toppled in recent memory), and so does the house to the left. The Academy has lost its widow's walk and spire, and has gained some additions on the west end, but the tower still rises above its roof.

CC

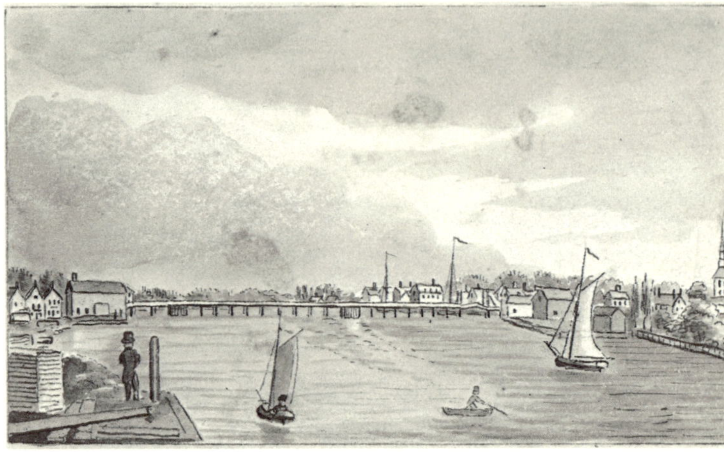

WESTPORT

SOUTH VIEW OF THE SAUGATUCK BRIDGE AND VILLAGE

102 THE SAUGATUCK RIVER is navigable farther north than any other waterway in Fairfield County. In 1811 Timothy Dwight wrote "At the head of navigation it is crossed by a bridge, around which is a neat, flourishing, and very pleasant village, built on both sides of the river, but principally on the eastern."

This bridge over the Saugatuck River was built in the early 19th century, replacing one built about 1798, and at the time that Barber sketched it, was part of the Connecticut Turnpike, a privately run toll road established to improve the old Boston Post Road. Four gates were set up between Fairfield and the New York line in Greenwich, one of which was here at this bridge. Tolls were collected until 1854 when the corporation was abandoned. The view is from down river looking north.

CC

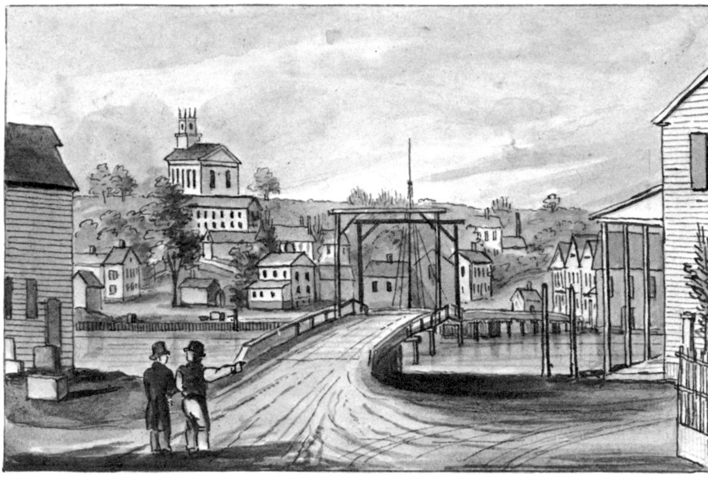

WESTPORT

VIEW IN THE CENTRAL PART

THIS IS A VIEW of the village of Saugatuck which was incorporated and named Westport the year Barber visited it in 1835. The Saugatuck River had been the boundary between Fairfield and Norwalk, but the community focused on water transport, and incorporation tied the two segments together.

Barber looks west towards the Episcopal church which had just been built the year before he drew this picture. On the far side of the bridge, at the right, is a small building which is probably 3 Riverside Avenue. It is thought to have been built in 1830, and since at least the 1940s has sheltered a package store.

The right foreground is the site of the present-day library, long the location of a store operated by Ebenezer Jesup, the grandfather of Morris Jesup who donated the land for the library in 1906.

CC

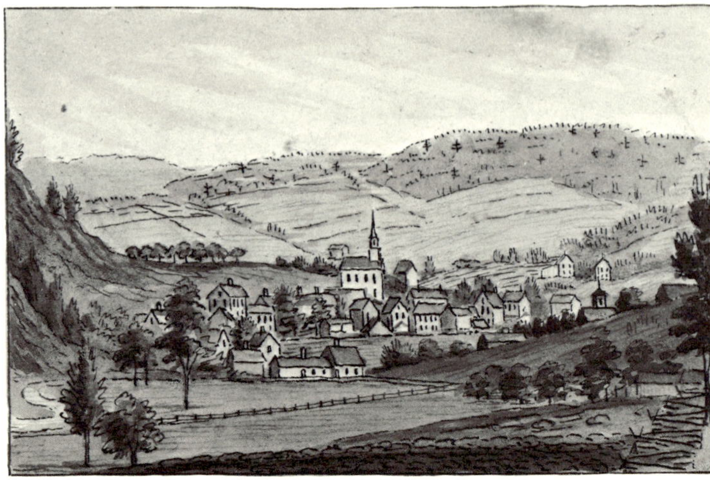

WINCHESTER

NORTH VIEW OF

THE BOROUGH OF CLIFTON

104 THE BOROUGH OF CLIFTON, previously known as West Village in Winsted, was incorporated in 1833. The village was built up in a narrow valley formed by the Still and Mad Rivers which created some of the state's best mill sites. The town boasts the earliest scythe factory in Connecticut and in 1835 Clifton featured several scythe factories and five forges. Barber described the community as "a flourishing village, consisting of about 60 or 70 dwelling houses and 4 mercantile stores." The view of the village looking south across Main Street shows the 1833 Methodist Church set well back from the road and with a grove of maple trees in front. According to one local historian, the church was built by nine trustees who showed "a greater capacity for managing dairy farms than for contracting and supervising the building of a church edifice." The church was replaced by a larger structure on High Street in 1900. A number of the houses shown in the view have survived. In the background of Barber's view can be seen a portion of the evergreen forest known as "Green Woods" that stretched across a substantial part of Litchfield County.

CPB

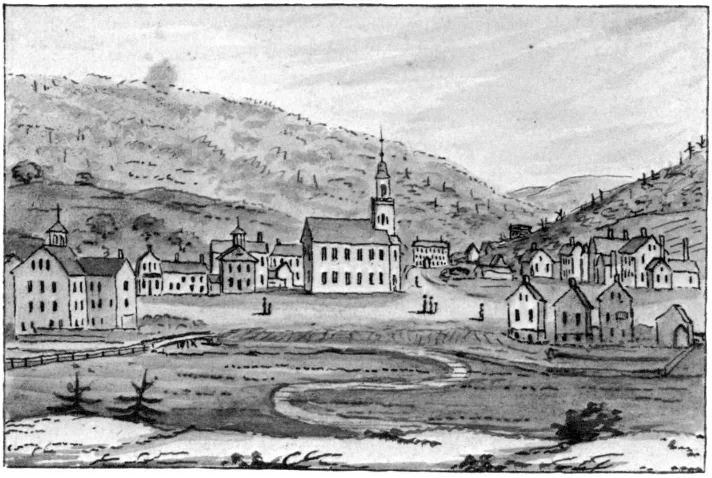

WINCHESTER

SOUTH VIEW OF THE VILLAGE OF WINSTED IN WINCHESTER

WHEN THE TOWN OF WINCHESTER was incorporated in 1771 there were only a few houses in Winsted, then known as East Village. The first meeting house in town was located in Winchester Center, several miles to the southwest. In 1799 Greenwoods Turnpike, close to the present Route 44, was opened and in 1800 a new Congregational church, the second in the East Village, was constructed on the Green in East Village. Barber's view, taken in October 1835, shows the church, an academy to the west, Winsted Tavern to the east, and several houses. None of these buildings survive. A Soldier's Monument erected in 1904 stands on the former site of the church in the middle of the Green. The Congregational Church was moved to a new location in 1848 and turned into a tenement in 1900 when a stone Congregational church was constructed on the north side of the Green.

CPB

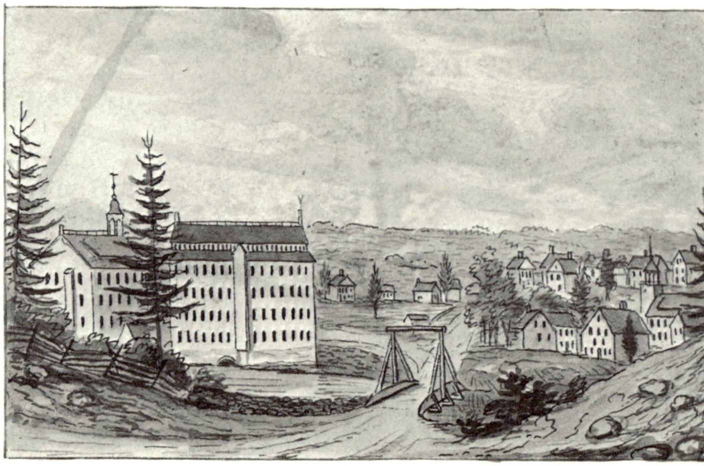

WINDHAM

SOUTHWEST VIEW OF WILLIMANTIC

THE ARTIST POSITIONED himself on a slight rise south of the village along the road (present Route 32) leading from Norwich to Willimantic, a location which gave Barber a fine view of the Windham Company cotton factory erected in the 1820s. A wooden bridge spanning the Willimantic River appears in the center of the image. The river, with a 91 foot drop, provided ample water power for other textile mills in the borough, and its course shaped the layout of the village. Today, the Willimantic River continues its dramatic course, but other features of Barber's view have long since been replaced. Buildings of the American Thread Company constructed in the late 19th century and among the largest factory structures in eastern Connecticut now line the river. Now closed, the buildings are being developed for commercial and residential use. The wooden bridge was replaced in the late 19th century by a stone and iron bridge. A railroad bridge now obscures Barber's line of sight, a reminder that Willimantic was a major railroad terminus 80 years ago. A newly opened textile museum and the planned relocation of a railroad museum signal a strong future for Willimantic's history.

CPB

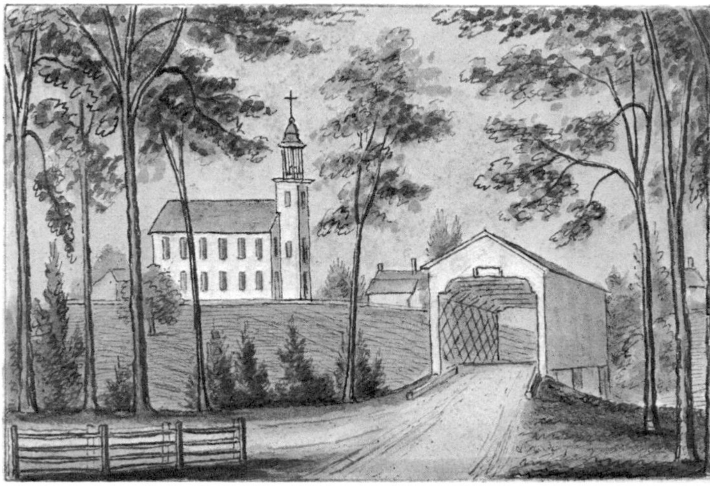

WINDSOR

SOUTH VIEW OF THE CONGREGATIONAL CHURCH

THE PRESENT BUILDING of the First Church in Windsor was designed and erected by architect Ebenezer Clark in 1794. It stands on Palisado Avenue, Route 159, along the north bank of the Farmington River. The original design, as shown by Barber, was altered to its present appearance in 1844, at which time the square tower and cupola were removed and replaced by a square architectural crown, and pillars were added to the front.

The wooden bridge, built in 1833, was carried away in the annual flood or "freshet" of 1854 and replaced by a second wooden bridge which was replaced by a steel bridge in 1919. The steel bridge is now (1989) being replaced and the "pleasant grove" of trees was cut down to provide space for this new construction.

The First Church in Windsor is considered "the oldest Congregational Church in America." The congregation was organized in March 1630, at Plymouth, England, before the members sailed for America. They settled in Dorchester, Massachusetts from 1630 to 1635 when the members began removing to Windsor where a Plymouth Trading Post had been established in 1633, making Windsor the first Connecticut town settled by English emigrants.

CLR

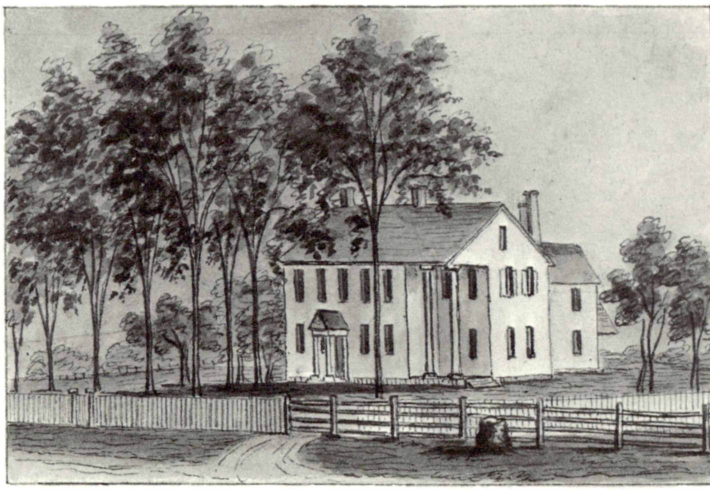

WINDSOR

SOUTHWEST VIEW OF

JUDGE ELLSWORTH'S HOUSE

THE OLIVER ELLSWORTH HOMESTEAD, 778 Palisado Avenue, is located on Route 159, about two miles north of the center of Windsor. The house was built in 1740 by Oliver's father, David Ellsworth. The original house is one of the earliest examples of central-hall architecture in Connecticut; Oliver Ellsworth added a large drawing room on the south with a two-story porch under an extension of the main roof. The house remained in the Ellsworth family until 1903, when ownership was transferred to the Connecticut Daughters of the American Revolution who now maintain it as a museum. Dutch elm disease has caused the removal of the elm trees in the front of the house.

Oliver Ellsworth, 1745–1807, was a Judge of the Connecticut Supreme Court, a member of the Council of Safety during the Revolutionary War, one of the framers of the Federal Constitution, a Minister Plenipotentiary to France, United States Senator, and the third Chief Justice of the Supreme Court of the United States.

CLR

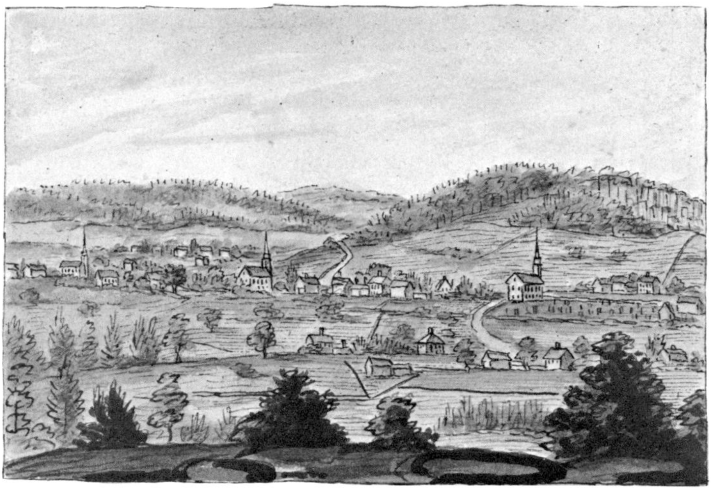

WOODBURY

SOUTHWEST VIEW

FROM BARE HILL

THE CENTER OF WOODBURY extends for several miles along present day Route 6 creating something of a dilemma for the artist. John Warner Barber wanted to find a vantage point which would allow him to include all of the most significant structures in the town. He placed himself on an elevation which he calls Bare (Bear) Hill from the black bears which are still sighted there. Looking down on the town in a northeasterly direction he could include the Glebe House to the right and the Episcopal, Methodist, and Congregational churches stretched out along Main Street, with steep hills in the distance. Everything appears in miniature and the churches had to be drawn from the rear, but the total effect, a conventional landscape composition, is quite successful.

Woodbury is one of the best preserved towns in the state. All of the important buildings in Barber's view are standing today. The restored Glebe House, where Samuel Seabury was elected bishop of the Church of England in America in 1783, is operated today as a house museum. The three churches have also been carefully maintained. The landscape, however, has undergone considerable change. The open meadows have been divided up into house lots, a symptom of the high price of land in Litchfield County.

CPB

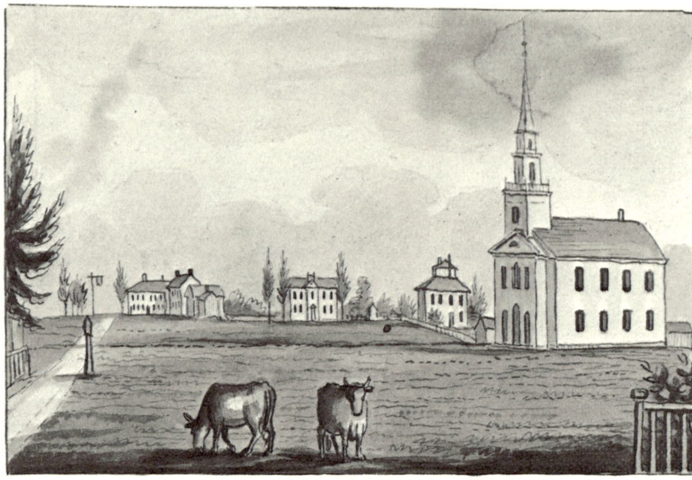

WOODSTOCK

SOUTH VIEW OF THE CONGREGATIONAL CHURCH

BARBER ARRIVED IN WOODSTOCK on the 27th of August, 1835 and sketched the town the following morning. He described the town as hilly, with fertile soil well suited to grazing, a feature which he emphasized by placing two cows in the middle of the common.

The center of South Woodstock has not changed radically from the time when Barber sat down to sketch the green. The First Congregational church, dedicated in 1823 and the third meeting house on the site, is well preserved and it continues to anchor the south end of the green. At the north end, Woodstock Academy, founded in 1801–02, now is spread out over several buildings. The original Academy building has been moved and erected elsewhere in town. The tavern seen in Barber's view just to the right of the Norwich and Worcester turnpike (now Route 169) remains in the same location but is now obscured by the town library. Roseland Cottage built by the Bowen family and now a house museum faces the green. Cows no longer graze on the green, but otherwise the town retains much of its rural quality and its widely-recognized beauty.

CPB

VIEWS IN VARIOUS TOWNSHIPS IN CONNECTICUT AND THE DAY ON WHICH JOHN WARNER BARBER TOOK EACH VIEW

NOTE: John Warner Barber included the following list of his town views of Connecticut in a manuscript notebook owned by the Fairfield Historical Society. It includes entries from the 1850s through the 1880s. It is remarkable that, in most cases, we know the exact day when Barber took the initial sketches from which the wood engraving—which he calls cuts—were made. Barber insisted on the essential accuracy of his views and requested his readers who questioned his reliability to place themselves in the same vantage point before judging him. Because in many instances these views represent the earliest depictions of Connecticut towns, it adds to the value of the image to know the precise day when Barber visited a town. The dates when he visited towns were extracted by Barber himself from the daily diary that he maintained from 1813 to 1885. The spelling and wording follow Barber's text. In those cases where no dates are provided, Barber's diary simply does not reveal the information.

Ashford	(central part) Church, Academy & 2 Taverns August 28, 1835
Avon	(central part) Baptist & Congregational Churches (Tower) Oct. 7, 1834
Barkhamsted	(Hitchcocksville) Church, Factories Sept. 3, 1835
Berlin	Village of Worthington, 3 churches &c. Oct. 2, 1835
Bethlem	(central part) Cong. and Episcopal Churches Aug. 1, 1835
Bloomfield	(central part) Cong. Ch. & other buildings Oct. 10, 1835
Bolton	Bolton stone quarry Oct. 11, 1834
Bridgeport	Large pl. or cut of the 4 churches. Large pl. City 1849. Churches July 9, 1834
Bozrah	Fitchville cotton fac. &c. Aug. 4, 1834
Bristol	Main village showing 3 churches Oct. 10, 1835
Brookfield	Central part; 2 churches, town ho &c. Nov. 5, 1835

Killingworth	Central part. Ship yard place Nov. 13, 1834
Lebanon	2 cuts Cong. Ch. Gov. Trumbull ho. & tomb June 3, 1835
Litchfield	Steel plate view of Litchfield Oct. 7, 1835
Old Lyme	2 cuts. Old Lyme vill. Gov. Griswold ho. Oct. 13, 1835
Madison	Lee's Academy & Cong. Church Nov. 13, 1834
Manchester	Methodist and Cong. Churches Aug. 29, 1835
Mansfield	Presbyterian Church Aug. 29, 1835
Meriden	2 cuts Ancient Churches, Cathole Pass July 1, 1834
Middletown	Steel pl. public buildings, Wesleyan. Aug. 11, 1836
Milford	2 cuts Cong. Churches; Oyster Huts May 20, 1834
Monroe	Central part. Episcopal & Cong. Ch. Academy Sept. 12, 1834
Montville	2 cuts Mohegan Ch. Occum House Aug. 4, 1834
New Canaan	Cong. & Episcopal Chs. Academy & Town House June 16, 1834
New Hartford	North Village Oct. 5, 1835
New Haven	Steel pl. Cuts. Ancient Ft. Hale, Yale Coll Hospital, West Rock & Westville, Fair Haven; Humphrey Monument, Ashmun do., and several smaller, no date
New London	Steel pl. Ft. Trumbull,—Judge Brainard's mon.—Bishop Seabury do. Hempstead Ho. no date
New Milford	Wide central street; churches &c. July 29, 1835

Newtown	Central part Churches &c. June 15, 1835
Norfolk	Central part. Congregational ch. &c. Oct. 7, 1835
North Haven	2 cuts Episcopal & Cong. Churches, Dr. Trumbull's ho. June 23, 1836
Norwalk	3 cuts Norwalk Borough,—Town Houses, Old Well July 7, 1834 and 1836
Norwich	Steel pl. Norwich City; 2 cuts: Central part of the town; factories at Yantic Falls Aug. 4, 1834
Oxford	Central part June, 1835
Plainfield	Congregational Church & Plainfield Academy Aug. 26, 1835
Preston	Poquetannuck village Aug. 4, 1834
Reading	Gen. Putnam's headquarters June 16, 1835
Ridgefield	Spot where Arnold met the British Sept. 11, 1835
Roxbury	Central part, Cong. & Episcopal churches July 28, 1835
Salisbury	Churches and Academy in the Center July 30, 1835
Saybrook	Lady Fenwick's Monument Nov. 14, 1834
Sharon	Gov. Smith's house July 30, 1835
Simsbury	Tariffville carpet manufacturing vill Oct. 8, 1834
Somers	Central part Sept. 1, 1835
Southbury	Mitchell House June 20, 1835
Southington	View of 3 churches in central part Oct. 9, 1835

Stafford	Mineral Springs Hotel &c. Oct. 16, 1835
Stamford	2 cuts—Stamford borough, Davenport. no date
Stratford	Episcopal Church April 3, 1835
Suffield	Connecticut Literary Institution Oct. 8, 1834
Stonington	Stonington Borough Aug. 1, 1834
Thompson	This village is on a commanding eminence as the center of the town Aug. 27, 1835
Tolland	Court house, Bank, Col. Smith tavern Baptist Church, jail. no date
Torrington	Wolcottville Village Nov. 8, 1834
Vernon	Congregational ch. & other buildings in the central part Oct. 16, 1834
Wallingford	Central part, churches, public buildings April 13, 1835
Waterbury	Central part, Baptist, Congregational & Episcopal ch. Oct. 8, 1835
Watertown	2 cuts. Trumbull ho. & Episcopal church Oct. 8, 1835
Weston	Congregational ch. and Academy June 1835
Westport	Bridge 40 rods long. Episcopal ch. June 14, 1836
Wethersfield	4 cuts. Map, State Prison, Webb Ho., Armorial of Chester Oct. 18, 1834
Winchester	2 cuts. Clifton Borough, Winsted Oct. 7, 1835
Windham	3 cuts. Ancient village, Frog pond, Willimantic borough Aug. 25, 1835

Windsor	4 cuts. Cong. Church & Bridge, Judge Ellsworth ho., Palisado plot, Wolcott mon. May 19, 1835
Woodbury	2 cuts. Bethel Rock, Fisher Hartshorn's grave Nov. 12, 1830
Woodstock	Cong. Church & Academy Aug. 28, 1835
West Hartford	Birthplace of Noah Webster Jan. 17, 1849

CHECKLIST OF JOHN WARNER BARBER PENCIL SKETCHES, INK WASHES, AND WOOD BLOCKS

The abbreviation "pag" refers to page references in the 1838 edition of *Connecticut Historical Collections*; "p" refers to the pencil sketches, "i" to the ink washes, and "w" to the woodblocks. C refers to The Connecticut Historical Society; Y refers to the Sterling Library, Yale University.

town	*location*	*pag*	*p*	*i*	*w*
Ashford	Southwestern view/central part	418	C	C	Y
Avon	East view of Avon		C		
Avon	East view of Avon		C		
Barkhamsted	West view of Hitchcockville	461	C	C	Y
Berlin	Northern view of Worthington	065	C	C	
Berlin	Worthington		C		
Bethlehem	South view, central part	462	C	C	Y
Bloomfield	S. view of Congregational Ch.	068	C	C	Y
Bloomfield	2nd view				
Bolton	Bolton Stone Quarry	543	C	C	Y
Bozrah	East view of Fitchville	301	C	C	
Branford	Central part./Cong., Epis. Ch.	189	C	C	Y
Bridgeport	City buildings		C		
Bridgeport	South view of Churches	373	C	C	C
Bridgeport	Stirling Hotel/range of stores		C		
Bridgeport	East view of Bridgeport, 1834	371	C	C	C
Bridgeport	S. view of Black Rock		C		
Bristol	Western view	069	C	C	Y
Brookfield	Northern view, central part	376	C	C	Y
Brooklyn	North view, central part	415	C		Y
Canaan	Canaan		C		
Canaan	SW view of Housatonic Falls	463	C	C	
Canaan	Falls		C		
Canterbury	South view, central part	421	C	C	Y
Canton	S. west view of Collinsville	071	C	C	Y
Chatham	Southern view of Episcopal Ch.	519	C	C	Y
Chatham	East view of Episcopal Church		C		
Cheshire	South view, central part.	194	C	C	
Cheshire	Episcopal Academy	195	C	C	
Chester	N. view, central part, 1837	522		C	Y
Colchester	Bacon Academy & Cong. Church	304	C	C	
Colebrook	S. west view, central part	465	C	C	Y
Collinsville	West view		C		

town	*location*	*pag*	*p*	*i*	*w*
Columbia	South view		C		
Cornwall	Foreign Mission School			C	
Cornwall	Northeastern view/S. Cornwall	466	C	C	Y
Coventry	North view of the Hale House	545	C	C	Y
Danbury	Congregational Ch. in Bethel	370	C	C	
Danbury	South view, central part	364	C	C	
Danbury	Southeastern view	363	C	C	
Danbury	Sandemanian Church	368	C	C	
Darien	Southwestern view/Cong. Church	377	C	C	
Derby	S. E. view		C		
Derby	Smithville		C	C	
Durham	Congregational Church		C	C	Y
East Haddam	Leesville		C		
East Haddam	West view of E.H. Landing	525	C	C	Y
East Haddam	S view/Mt. Tom/mouth/Salmon R.	527	C		
East Haddam	Mt. Tom/Salmon River/E. Haddam		C		
East Haddam	Mechanicsville		C		
East Hartford	N. view, E. Hartford Cong. ch.		C		
East Hartford	2nd view/S. view in E. Htfd st.		C		
East Haven	S. part of Saltonstall Pond		C		
East Haven	Cong. & Episc. Churches	205	C	C	Y
Ellington	Western view, central part	549	C	C	Y
Enfield	Shaker houses	085	C	C	
Enfield	Shaker Meeting House no. 2		C		
Enfield	Thompsonville	084	C	C	Y
Fairfield	W. view of Buckley Tavern			C	
Fairfield	Court house/Cong. Church/jail	353	C	C	
Fairfield	Greenfield Hill		C		
Fairfield	2nd view		C	C	
Fairfield	S. view, Borough of Southport	356	C	C	
Farmington	NW view from Round Hill	089	C	C	Y
Glastonbury	Glastenbury Church		C		
Glastonbury	Cotton Factory village	092	C	C	Y
Goshen	South view, central part	468	C	C	Y
Granby	S vw. of Newgate Prison Bldgs.	094	C	C	
Greenwich	SE view of Putnam's Hill	381	C	C	
Groton	Groton Heights		C		
Groton	Groton Monument & Ft. Griswold	310	C	C	
Groton	North view of Pequot Hill	312	C	C	
Groton	Portersville & Lower Mystic	308	2	C	
Groton	S vw. of Porter's Rock, Mystic		C		
Groton	Northeastern view of Fort Hill	317	C	C	Y
Groton	Groton Monument		C		Y
Groton	South view of Porter's Rock	313	C	C	Y

town	*location*	*pag*	*p*	*i*	*w*
Guilford	Congregational Church	213	C	C	Y
Guilford	Congreg. & Episcopal Churches				
Guilford	Ancient House #106	212	C	C	
Haddam	Birthplace of David Brainerd	517	C	C	Y
Haddam	Northwest view	516	C	C	Y
Hamden	Central part	219	C	C	Y
Hamden	South view of Whitneyville	220	C	C	Y
Hartford	1st Meeting House built in CT	042		C	Y
Hartford	Th. Hooker house			C	
Hartford	map of Htfd/Wethersfield line			C	
Hartford	Washington College				Y
Hartford	Hooker House			C	
Hartford	Charter Oak in Winter		C		
Hartford	East view of Hartford		C		
Hartford	Hartford Bridge		C		Y
Hartland	S. east view of Hartland		C		
Hebron	South view, central part	550	C	C	
Huntington	S. view/Epis. & Cong. Churches	383	C	C	Y
Jewett City	S. view, about a mile distant		C		Y
Kent	NE view, Episcopal Church	470	C	C	C
Killingly	Western view of Danielsonville	433	C	C	Y
Killingworth	West view, central part	530	C	C	Y
Lebanon	Tomb of the Trumbull Family	324	C	C	
Lebanon	War office & Gov. Trumbull ho.		C		
Lebanon	"Lebanon South or SE"		C		
Lyme	S. view/Gov. Griswold's House	330	C		C
Lyme	West view of Lyme	329	C	C	Y
Madison	Lee's Academy & Cong. Church	224	C	C	Y
Manchester	Union Manufacturing		C		
Manchester	Methodist & Cong. Churches	099	C	C	Y
Mansfield	NE view of Presbyterian Church	552	C	C	
Meriden	North view of Cat Hole pass	228	C	C	
Meriden	Cold Spring Meri[den]		C		
Meriden, churches in	Southern view of the Churches	227	C	C	
Middletown	Public Buildings in central pt	509	C	C	
Middletown	East view				
Middletown	N. view				
Milford	S. view of 2 Cong. Churches	234		C	Y
Milford	Oyster Huts on Milford Point	238		C	
Milford	Milford		C		
Monroe	S. view of Churches in Monroe		C		
Monroe	Episcopal church		C		
Montville	South view of Mohegan Chapel	339	C	C	
Montville	Sampson Occum house in Mohegan	340	C	C	Y

town	*location*	*pag*	*p*	*i*	*w*
Morris Cove	South east Morris Cove		C		
New Britain	Northern view of New Britain		C		
New Britain	North east		C		
New Britain	North West view, central part.	067	C	C	
New Canaan	East view				Y
New Hartford	Northern view, North Village	473	C	C	
New Haven	South view & Fort Hale				C
New Haven	Yale College	145	C		C
New Haven	S view of Fair Haven/west part	158	C	C	C
New Haven	Judges Cave, Westville		C		C
New Haven	Westville & West Rock	150	C		
New Haven	New Haven Light Ho.				
New London	Judge Brainard's Monument	281		C	
New London	North view of Fort Trumbull		C		
New London	View from Groton		C		
New London	S view/N London & Ft. Trumbull	272	C		
New London	Bishop Seabury's Monument	282	C	C	C
New London	South view of Hempstead House	283	C	C	Y
New London	Hallam family tomb		C		
New Milford	South view, central part	479	C	C	Y
Newgate prison	Newgate Prison—dr. by Willard		C		
Newtown	Sandy Hook		C		
Newtown	South view	388	C	C	
Newtown	Episcopal church		C		
Norfolk	East view, central part	482	C	C	Y
Norfolk	East view of Norfolk		C		
North Haven	2 churches in New Haven		C		
North Haven	Congregational Church	242	C	C	Y
North Haven	N. view of Congregational ch.		C		
Norwalk	S. view, Norwalk Town House	391	2		Y
Norwalk	E view of village of Old Well	393	C	C	C
Norwalk	South view	390	C	C	C
Norwich	Eastern view, central part	292	C	C	Y
Norwich	Rocky Pt. Norwich		C		
Norwich	South view of Norwich		C		
Norwich	2nd view		C		
Oxford	Southeastern view/central part	248	C	C	Y
Plainfield	Western view	435	C	C	Y
Plymouth	East view, central part	483	C	C	Y
Pomfret	Putnam's Wolf Den	439		C	
Preston?	Pocatonnuc Preston		C		
Reading	House/form. Gen. Putnam's HQ	395	C	C	Y
Ridgefield	View in Ridgefield				C
Ridgefield	N. view of Presbyterian Church		C		

town	*location*	*pag*	*p*	*i*	*w*
Rocky Hill	View of Quarry, Silliman lith.	039		C	Y
Roxbury	Northeastern view, central part	485	C	C	Y
Salisbury	SW view of chs. in S. center		C		
Salisbury	Salisbury Center		C		
Sandy Hook	(Newton) S. view of Sandy Hook		C		
Saybrook	NE view of Borough of Essex	534	C	C	Y
Saybrook	Fenwick Mon.		C		C
Saybrook?	Saybrook Point		C		
Saybrook?	Saybrook Pt. 2nd		C		
Sharon	South view, Gov. Smith's House	491	C	C	Y
Sharon	Gov. Smith's house		C		
Simsbury	South view of Tariffville	101	C	C	Y
Simsbury	Newgate Prison		C		
Somers	West view		C		
Somers	West view, central part	554	C	C	Y
South Britain	South Britain, Southbury		C		
South Windsor	Theological Institute of CT	077		C	Y
Southbury	Mitchell's Mansion House	251	C		Y
Southbury	Mitchell's House				
Southington	South view, central part.	105	C	C	Y
Southport	South view	411	C	C	
Stamford	Southwestern view	403	C	C	C
Stratford	S.E. view/Episcopal Church	406	C	C	C
Suffield	CT Literary Institution	108		C	
Suffield	S. view of Suffield		C		
Suffield	2nd view, north view		C		
Suffield	Suffield school and church		C		
Thompson	South view, central part	442	C	C	Y
Tolland	South view, central part	541	C	C	Y
Torrington	Northeastern view/Wolcottville	496	C	C	Y
Trumbull	N. view/Ft. Trumbull from N.L.	273	2		
Union	N. W. view		C		
Wallingford			C		
Wallingford	Central part	254	C	C	
Warren	East view, central part			C	
Waterbury	Southeastern view		C		
Waterford	Baptist Church		C		
Waterford	Beckwith house, Waterford		C		
Watertown	North view of Trumbull House	500		C	Y
Watertown	Southern view, central part			C	
Watertown	Trumbull house w/public bldgs.		C		
Watertown	NE view, central part	499	C	C	
West Haven	Savin Rock				
Westbrook	Northwestern view of Westbrook		C		

town	*location*	*pag*	*p*	*i*	*w*
Weston	Cong. Church & the Academy	410	C	C	C
Westport	Central part				C
Westport	Saugatuck bridge	nn	C	C	
Wethersfield	Webb House/G. Washington House	116	C		Y
Wethersfield	S. view of Congregational ch.		C		
Winchester	North view of Clifton	502	C	C	Y
Winchester	North view of Winsted	503	C	C	Y
Windham	View of Willimantic				
Windham	Easterm view of Windham	444			Y
Windham	Southwestern view of Frog Pond	447			Y
Windham	South view of Willimantic	446	C	C	Y
Windsor	Palisado	132		C	
Windsor	SW view Judge Ellsworth's House	129	C	C	Y
Windsor	South view of Congr. Church	124	C	C	Y
Windsor?	Wolcott Mon. Windsor				
Woodbury	Castle rock		C		
Woodbury	Woodbury from Bare Hill		C	C	
Woodbury	Monument/Grave of F. Hartshorn	505	C	C	Y
Woodbury	Southeast view of Bethel Rock	505	C	C	Y
Woodstock	South view of Congr. Church	450	C	C	Y

1500 copies have been printed by
Meriden-Stinehour Press, Lunenburg, Vt.
on 70 lb. Mohawk Vellum text, Cream White,
and the endleaves are Mohawk Vellum text, Sandstone.
The binding in Holliston Roxite B Cloth is by
Acme Bindery, Charleston, Mass.
The book is designed by
John O. C. McCrillis.

ACORN CLUB

MEMBERS

Richard G. Akeroyd, Jr., *South Windsor*
Christopher P. Bickford, *Canterbury*
Dorothy W. Bridgwater, *Hamden*
Christopher Collier, *Orange*
John M. K. Davis, *Bloomfield*
Ralph Gregory Elliot, *West Hartford*
Donald B. Engley, *Bloomfield*
James F. English, Jr., *West Hartford*
Bruce Fraser, *Middletown*
Ellsworth S. Grant, *West Hartford*
Thompson R. Harlow, *Newington*
Oliver O. Jensen, *Old Saybrook*
John P. McDonald, *Storrs*
J. Bard McNulty, *Glastonbury*
David F. Musto, *New Haven*
John C. Parsons, *Hartford*
Henry H. Pierce, *New Haven*
Cedric L. Robinson, *Windsor*
Brian Rogers, *Mystic*
Floyd M. Shumway, *New Haven*
Edward Sloan, *Hartford*
Gaddis Smith, *New Haven*
Glenn Weaver, *Wethersfield*

HONORARY MEMBERS

Herman W. Liebert, *New Haven*
Marshall H. Montgomery, *Del Ray Beach, Florida*
Wyman W. Parker, *Middlebury, Vermont*
Willard M. Wallace, *Berlin*